手绘名物系列
Hand - Drawn Classic Travel Landmarks

中国古桥

Ancient Chinese Bridges

管维 沈晓雷 文
Written by Guan Wei amd Shen Xiaolei

蔡频春 绘
Illustrated by Cai Pinchun

姜琳 译
Translated by Jiang Lin

中国画报出版社·北京
China Pictorial Press · Beijing

图书在版编目（CIP）数据

中国古桥：汉英对照 / 管维，沈晓雷文；蔡频春绘；姜琳译. -- 北京：中国画报出版社，2023.4
（手绘名物系列）
ISBN 978-7-5146-2067-2

Ⅰ.①中… Ⅱ.①管… ②沈… ③蔡… ④姜… Ⅲ.①古建筑—桥介绍—中国—汉、英 Ⅳ.①K928.78

中国版本图书馆CIP数据核字(2022)第039821号

中国古桥（汉英对照）

管维 沈晓雷 文
蔡频春 绘

出 版 人：方允仲
项目主持：方允仲　齐丽华
责任编辑：齐丽华　李聚慧
英文翻译：姜　琳
英文编辑：王子木
责任印制：焦　洋

出版发行：中国画报出版社
地　　址：中国北京市海淀区车公庄西路33号　邮编：100048
发 行 部：010-88417360　010-68414683（传真）
总编室兼传真：010-88417359　版权部：010-88417359

开　　本：16开（787mm×1092mm）
印　　张：10.75
字　　数：120千字
版　　次：2023年4月第1版　2023年4月第1次印刷
印　　刷：北京汇瑞嘉合文化发展有限公司
书　　号：ISBN 978-7-5146-2067-2
定　　价：108.00元

前言

本书是"大美中国"书系中的一本。顾名思义，所谓"大美"，无外乎自然界和人类社会中，具有高度审美价值的客体、对象。它们可以是自然界中的山川河流，可以是花鸟虫鱼，也可能是风雨雷电、莺歌燕舞，更有可能是通过色彩、线条、声音、文字等人文艺术表现出来的各种艺术形式，如音乐、舞蹈、建筑、书法、绘画、雕塑、戏剧、电影等。而这些，都来源于东方古老的文明大国——中国。

浑浊而奔腾不息的黄河孕育了古老的华夏文明。中国人的先祖从母亲河走来，由部落壮大成为部落国家，从王国跨越到帝国，经历了漫长的封建时代。最终，在近代的数次实践之后，中国走上了社会主义新中国的道路——在这漫长的历史中，有统一，也有分裂；有强盛，也有衰败。部落演进为国家的历史，中国经历了一千多年，封土建国的周朝，前后存在了八百多年，之后漫长的封建时期，历时两千余年才告结束——可中国的历史，却又不止于长：不仅长，还富于变化。中国五千多年的文明和国家史，从来不是一成不变的：在四千余年的建国史中，中国经历了约十五个朝代，六七十个政权交替更迭，更见证了不计其数的大小战争——战争和政权更替固然给人民带来了深重的灾难，却又在客观上催动着社会生活方方面面的变化，为中国展开了一幅波澜壮阔的历史图卷；从天文、历算到农耕器具的进步，从造纸、印刷到选官制度的变化、商业的繁荣，中华民族就这样一步步走来，走到今天。

Foreword

This book is part of the "Beautiful China" book series. As its name implies, the book series focuses on depicting objects of high aesthetical value in nature and human society. They include not only creatures such as birds, beasts, insects and fish but also natural phenomena such as wind, rain, thunder and lightning. They may also be various forms of art composed with colors, lines, sound and texts, such as music, dance, architecture, calligraphy, painting, sculpture, drama, and movie. Regardless of their form, all of them derive from China, an ancient civilization in the East.

The muddy, ceaseless flow of the Yellow River fostered the ancient Chinese civilization. Nourished by the "mother river", Chinese ancestors gradually developed their tribes into tribal nations, then kingdoms and empires across the feudal era. Eventually, after several attempts of practical exploration in modern times, China embarked on a path of socialism with Chinese characteristics. Throughout its long history, China experienced unifications and separations as well as ups and downs. The history of tribal nations in China lasted for more than 1,000 years, followed by the Zhou dynasty (1046-256 BC) that spanned about 800 years. Then, China entered the feudal period as long as more than 2,000 years. However, the course of China's history is more than just long; it is also full of changes. Across its history of more than 5,000 years, the Chinese civilization has never stopped the pace of evolution. Throughout its history of more than 4,000 years as a nation state, China fostered 15 dynasties and some 70 regimes, and underwent numerous wars. Of course, wars and regime shifts might bring grave disasters to the people, but at the same time they accelerated changes in all aspects of society and composed the eventful picture of Chinese history. From progress in astronomy, calendrical science and farming tools, and improvements in printing and papermaking techniques

前言
Foreword

习近平主席曾多次指出,"当今世界正经历百年未有之大变局";正是在这样的时代机遇和文化背景下,中国外文局责成中国画报出版社推出了"大美中国"这个书系。本书系既是对中国自然、风物、人文的总结,也是为了向全世界关心中国、热爱中国、崇敬中国的人讲好中国故事。

但凡讲故事,必要有一个主题,有一个入口;我们选择向世界展现中国之美,这并非任意为之。人们总是喜欢美好的东西,这非但是中国人民的追求,也是全世界各国人民、各个民族的追求——不同文化对美的定义或许不同,可这追求却是一致的,而且古来有之。

中国之美既有历史的深邃厚重,又有地域的辽远广阔。大到富丽繁华的都市,小到鲜有问津的村镇,历史总会在这里那里,留下星星点点的痕迹。地域的辽阔又为中国之美赋予了不同的风格。我们既有高山大川,又有小桥流水;既有高屋广厦,又有陋室闲庭;既有"长河落日圆"的雄壮,又有"清泉石上流"的清丽……疆土有多少寸,美就有多少种,简直是说也说不尽的。以自然地理和城镇乡村为依托,我们更想展现一种人文的厚度,南北东西、平原山地、沿海内陆……不同地方的人,

and official selection systems to prosperity of commerce, the Chinese nation have constantly moved forward step by step to the present day.

Chinese President Xi Jinping said on many occasions that the world is undergoing "profound changes unseen in a century." Facing such historic opportunities and cultural context, under the instruction of China International Communications Group, China Pictorial Press presented the "Beautiful China" book series, which not only reviews the natural and cultural sights of China but also tells China's stories to global readers who care, love and admire China.

A story needs a theme or a topic. We do not casually choose "Beautiful China" as the theme of the stories we try to tell. All people love beautiful things. In fact, the pursuit of beauty represents the common aspiration of not only the Chinese people but also people from other parts of the world. The definition of beauty may differ for different cultures, but people around the world have had a shared aspiration for beauty since ancient times.

The beauty of China stems from its profound history and vast territory. Whether in spectacular, prosperous metropolises or in nondescript small towns, we can always find clues left by history. The diverse cultures scattered around the country's vast territory bestow on China different types of beauty. There are high mountains and big rivers as well as exquisite bridges and murmuring streams; there are skyscraping buildings as well as simple dwellings; there are magnificent views of torrential rivers in the setting sun as well as elegant sights of clear streams flowing through rocks… The beauty of China is just as boundless as its territory. With this book, we would like to show readers the natural geography and cultural profundity of various cities, towns and villages across China, from plains to mountains and from coastal areas to inland areas, as well as how people in different regions live in

他们都在以什么样的方式生活着,他们的生活有何不同,而这种种生活又如何共同构成了中国的文化和民生的一部分。一言以蔽之,我们想要传达的,不是某种抽象的概念,不是简单的意象或标准化的符号,而是由真实、具体的细节所构成的鲜活的生活与生命。

本书系通过文图作品讲述中国故事,以画面语言为主,辅以文字的叙述、解释和说明,向读者传递更完善的印象和更系统的知识。

除了摄影作品,我们还将绘画艺术融入到书系当中。例如"手绘名物系列",我们选择了通过水彩画的方式去讲述城市及其民俗的故事,这不仅构成了对城市的刻画,同时也是一次上好的艺术和美学教育。选择水彩画这一既为亚洲也为欧美所熟悉的艺术表现形式,去讲述城市这一最为大多数人所熟悉的生活空间,这是由于我们想以此作为出发点,把中国故事讲好,走近听众,把故事讲得生动真实、可闻可感。

沿着这样的轨迹,我们希望把中国最美的一面展示给世界,也想把中国的故事讲给全世界每一个喜欢她的人听。

different ways and how their lives together compose the country's diverse cultures and lifestyles. In one word, we intend to reveal the vigor of life through true and specific details, rather than an abstract concept, a simple imagery or a standardized symbol.

This book series tells stories about China through vivid pictures and language. Therefore, it prioritizes images, supplemented with textural narrations, explanations and remarks, so as to enable readers to obtain deeper impressions and systematic knowledge.

In addition to photographic works, we also incorporate painting into the book series. For example, the "Hand-Drawn Classic Travel Landmarks" sub-series feature hand-drawn watercolor illustrations depicting cities and their folk customs. This is not only an ideal way to portray cities, but also provides a chance for art and aesthetic education. Watercolor is a form of art familiar to readers around the world. We chose this form of art to portray cities, a kind of living spaces familiar to most people, in an effort to tell China's stories in a vivid, perceptible way and make them closer to readers.

By doing so, we hope to show the most beautiful side of China to the world and tell China's stories to every reader who is interested in the country and its culture.

目录 Contents

前言 Foreword

第一章 Chapter 1
匠心——古桥营造典范之作
Ingenuity——Quintessence of Ancient Bridges

01 永济桥
　　The Yongji Bridge 002

02 安平桥
　　The Anping Bridge 004

03 洛阳桥
　　The Luoyang Bridge 006

04 泸定桥
　　The Luding Bridge 008

05 赵州桥
　　The Zhaozhou Bridge 010

06 卢沟桥
　　The Lugou Bridge 012

07 五亭桥
　　The Five-Pavilion Bridge 014

08 五音桥
　　The Five-Pitches Bridge 016

09 鱼沼飞梁
　　Flying Bridge Across Yu Zhao 018

10 广济桥
　　The Guangji Bridge 020

第二章 Chapter 2

聚美——古镇桥群
A Gathering Place of Beautiful Scenes
—Cluster of Ancient Bridges in Ancient Towns

绍兴古桥群
The Shaoxing Ancient Bridge Cluster

01 泾口桥、太平桥、接渡桥
　　The Jingkou Bridge, the Taiping Bridge and the Jiedu Bridge 024

02 八字桥
　　The Bazi Bridge.. 026

03 纤道桥
　　The Qiandao Bridge 028

04 广宁桥
　　The Guangning Bridge 030

05 题扇桥、拜王桥
　　The Tishan Bridge and the Baiwang Bridge 032

06 光相桥、谢公桥
　　The Guangxiang Bridge and the Xiegong Bridge 034

07 泗龙桥
　　The Silong Bridge 036

故宫金水桥
The Golden Water Bridges in the Palace Museum

01 外金水桥
　　The Outer Golden Water Bridge 038

02 内金水桥
　　The Inner Golden Water Bridge... 040

德清古桥群
The Deqing Ancient Bridge Cluster

01 寿昌桥、永安桥
　　The Shouchang Bridge and the Yong'an Bridge 042

02 万寿桥
　　The Wanshou Bridge 044

03 普济桥
　　The Puji Bridge 046

04 社桥、青云桥、兼济桥
　　The Sheqiao Bridge, the Qingyun Bridge and the Jianji Bridge 048

沁江古桥群
The Bijiang River Ancient Bridge Cluster

01 青云桥
  The Qingyun Bridge 050

02 中州桥
  The Zhongzhou Bridge 052

03 安澜桥、阳春桥、永镇桥
  The Anlan Bridge, the Yangchun Bridge and the Yongzhen Bridge 054

04 通京桥
  The Tongjing Bridge 056

05 藤桥
  The Vine Bridges 058

06 彩凤桥
  The Caifeng Bridge 060

西湖古桥群
The West Lake Ancient Bridge Cluster

01 映波桥、锁澜桥
  The Yingbo Bridge and the Suolan Bridge 062

02 望山桥、压堤桥、跨虹桥
  The Wangshan Bridge, the Yadi Bridge and the Kuahong Bridge 064

03 断桥
  The Broken Bridge 066

04 长桥
  The Long Bridge 068

05 锦带桥
  The Jindai Bridge 070

06 通利桥
  The Tongli Bridge 072

泰顺廊桥
The Taishun Veranda Bridges

01 北涧桥
  The Beijian Bridge 074

02 溪东桥
  The Xidong Bridge 076

03 仙居桥、三条桥
  The Xianju Bridge and the Santiao Bridge 078

04 刘宅桥、普宾桥、墩头桥、薛宅桥
  The Liuzhai Bridge, the Pubin Bridge, the Duntou Bridge and the Xuezhai Bridge 080

05 永庆桥、霞光桥、南溪桥
  The Yongqing Bridge, the Xiaguang Bridge and the Nanxi Bridge 082

第三章 Chapter 3

卧虹——古城名桥
The Lying Rainbow——Famous Bridges in Ancient Cities

01 清名桥
    The Qingming Bridge 086

02 思本桥
    The Siben Bridge 088

03 宝带桥
    The Baodai Bridge 090

04 迎仙桥
    The Yingxian Bridge 092

05 江东桥
    The Jiangdong Bridge 094

06 太仓石拱桥
    The Taicang Stone Arch Bridges 096

07 都江堰南桥
    The South Bridge of Dujiangyan 098

08 青岛栈桥
    The Qingdao Zhanqiao Bridge 100

09 双龙桥
    The Double Dragon Bridge 102

10 龙脑桥
    The Longnao Bridge 104

11 清华彩虹桥
    The Qinghua Rainbow Bridge 106

12 安澜索桥
    The Anlan Cable Bridge 108

13 方顺桥
    The Fangshun Bridge 110

14 银锭桥
    The Yinding Bridge 112

15 波日桥
    The Bori Bridge 114

16 琉璃河石桥
    The Stone Bridge over the Liuli River 116

17 永通桥
    The Yongtong Bridge 118

18 卞桥
    The Bianqiao Bridge 120

19 永镇桥
    The Yongzhen Bridge 122

20 地坪风雨桥
    The Diping Fengyu Bridge 124

21 葛镜桥
    The Gejing Bridge 126

22 襄垣永惠桥
    The Xiangyuan Yonghui Bridge 128

23 毓秀桥
    The Yuxiu Bridge 130

24 双林三桥
    The Shuanglin Three Bridges 132

第四章 Chapter 4

静观——名园胜景中的古桥
Viewing in Still——Ancient Bridges in Famous Scenic Spots

颐和园中的桥
The Bridges in the Summer Palace
01 十七孔桥
    The Seventeen-Arch Bridge 136
02 玉带桥
    The Jade Belt Bridge 138

北海二桥
Two Bridges in Beihai
01 永安桥
    The Yong'an Bridge 140
02 金鳌玉蝀桥
    The Jin'ao Yudong Bridge 142

苏州园林诸桥
The Bridges in the Classical Gardens of Suzhou

01 九曲桥
The Jiuqu Bridge 144

02 小飞虹
The Small Flying Rainbow Bridge 146

03 引静桥
The Yinjing Bridge 148

其他桥
Other Bridges

01 庐山观音桥
The Guanyin Bridge in Mount Lu... 150

02 曲尺桥
The Quchi Bridge... 152

03 虎丘双井桥
The Shuangjing Bridge in Tiger Hill 154

第一章
Chapter 1

匠心
Ingenuity

古桥营造典范之作
Quintessence of Ancient Bridges

永济桥
The Yongji Bridge

广西三江侗族自治县程阳村,有一座雄伟壮观、闻名中外的廊桥——永济桥。廊桥因其桥面设有遮风挡雨的桥廊亦被称为"风雨桥"。永济桥初建时一无图纸,二无模型,整个建筑无钉无铁,仅凭当地人称为"香杆"的木角尺量画后,用凿榫衔接建成此桥。古桥集廊、亭、塔三者于一身,在中外建筑史上独具风韵。多雨潮湿的南方,木桥易受风雨侵袭而损毁,所以人们在桥上建造亭台楼阁,不仅可以阻挡风雨,也可以起到对桥梁结构的配重作用,使桥梁更能经受极端气候下的暴雨洪水冲击。日常中人们又可以借桥梁的交通枢纽作用聚集人气,便于附近居民在此从事商业活动,颇似如今大都市中各处地铁交通枢纽附近的繁华商业区。年复一年流水般的过客来往于坚若磐石的永济桥上,古桥在壮丽的山水与热闹的侗族寨子间熠熠生辉,于无声处见证着侗族乡寨的如画山水、烟火人家。

The Yongji Bridge, a majestic, world-known veranda bridge, erects in Chengyang Village, Sanjiang Dong Autonomous County of Guangxi Zhuang Autonomous Region. Veranda bridges are also called Fengyu bridges, meaning they can provide people shelters from "fengyu"—wind and rain—with their verandas. The Yongji Bridge was built in the approach of mortise and tenon without using any metal. The construction does not rely on any blue prints or models, only the data measured by a type of angle squares locally called "the fragrant pole." The ancient bridge integrates the features of veranda, pavilion and pagoda with unique charm in the Chinese and foreign architectural history. Wooden bridges are vulnerable to damages due to wind and rain in rainy and damp South China. So, people built pavilions, terraces and towers which could not merely shelter wind and rain but play the role of ballasting as the dynamic structure of the bridge so that the bridge could withstand the impact of storm and flood under extreme weather. Functioning as a transportation hub, people gather at Yongji Bridge, making it a perfect spot for residents nearby engaging commercial activities, just like those bustling commercial centers near underground transportation hubs in modern metropolises. This ancient bridge sits here, stiff as a rock, in this magnificient landscape, among the lively villages of the Dong people, watching people come and go, witnessing the picturesque scenery and the world of the motals of the Dong villages in silent, adding radiance to the world.

02 安平桥
The Anping Bridge

  泉州城外的海湾古称"安平遂",安平桥因位于此地而得名,又因桥长五里,亦称"五里桥",时人更是留下了"天下无桥长此桥"的评价。宋元时期泉州海外贸易的繁盛使万国货物云集于此,彼时的中国,多元的社会结构使得上自皇室贵胄、地方官绅,下至僧众商贾、居民百姓,共同修建了这座当时最长的跨海梁式石桥。古桥东端有亭,西端有庵,桥面上每隔一段距离亦有各式精致的亭、楼、塔。这些桥身建筑姿态各异,各有功用,有作为海港航标塔的白塔,也有用于行人观景小憩的听潮亭。徜徉于斑驳沧桑的古桥条石之上,已不见古代海上丝绸之路行船至此时万国高船巨帆汇聚的熙攘繁华,只见宁静的水面波澜微皱,一派洗尽铅华后的端方雅正。举目远眺桥面蜿蜒无尽,桥旁古塔、石狮尽收眼中,不知不觉间人已浸润于宏大广博的历史之中。

  The bay outside Quanzhou where the Anping Bridge is located was called "Anpingsui" in ancient China and the bridge got the name because of the place. The Anping Bridge is also called the Wu Li Bridge for it is five li (2,500 metres) long. It is acclaimed that "no other bridges are longer than this one." Commodities were transported from overseas to Quanzhou for transactions in the Song and Yuan dynasties. The diverse social structures of China integrated the royal family, nobles, local officers, monks, merchants and ordinary people as one to jointly build the worldwide longest beam stone bridge over the sea at that time. The ancient bridge boasts a pavilion in the east, a nunnery in the west and exquisite pavilions, towers and pagodas of all kinds at an interval on the bridge surface. The architectures on the bridge feature different postures and functions, including the white tower as a beacon tower for navigation and the Tide-Hearing Pavilion for the passersby to enjoy the view and have a rest. The past bustle and prosperity of large vessels from other countries via the Maritime Silk Road in ancient times disappeared from the stone strips of the mottled ancient bridge, only leaving the wrinkled waves on the tranquil water surface and an upright, elegant presence. Looking into the distance, you can see an endlessly winding bridge surface. With the ancient pagodas and the stone lions near the bridge in full view, you have been unconsciously immersed in the grand, profound history.

03 洛阳桥
The Luoyang Bridge

　　洛阳桥又名万安桥，位于古城泉州，始建于宋代，是中国第一座跨海梁式石桥。古时泉州曾是海上丝绸之路的重要港口，街巷路桥都满载历史的传奇。这里曾经中外货船帆樯林立，世界各国的商贾货物与繁忙贸易使得洛阳桥应运而生。刺桐花开的季节闲步桥上，脚步落在错落有致的宋代石板上，耳边回荡不绝的是千年足音，俯身望去，一座座形如小船的桥基承托着坚固的桥墩，周围满是白色斑驳的层层牡蛎。海水潮起潮落，朝代几番更迭，而洛阳桥却能够跨越千年，屹立如初，竟也有这小小牡蛎的功劳。古人种蛎固基，将人类的建筑与自然界的生物特性完美融合。粼粼波光中，未及感叹先人智慧高妙，便有白鹭掠过，翩然而去，将水中的亭塔倒影——漾开，一阵海水的微咸气息扑面而来，将你神游千年的思绪带回眼前。

The Luoyang Bridge, also called Wan'an Bridge, located in ancient city of Quanzhou, originally built in the Song dynasty (1127–1279), is the first beam stone bridge over the seas in China. In ancient times, Quanzhou was an important port of the Maritime Silk Road. The streets, alleys, roads and bridges there composed the legend of the history. Chinese and foreign cargo ships once perched there and the busy transactions of commodities from all over the world gave rise to the building of Luoyang Bridge. When you step leisurely on the well-spaced stones of the Song dynasty on the pedestrian bridge in the season when oriental variegated coralbean flowers come into bloom, you can hear the footsteps reverberating at your ears. Overlooked, boat-shaped foundations bear solid piers with white, mottled oysters scattered around. The Luoyang Bridge can erect still today after hundreds of years seeing the ebbs and flows of the sea and successions of different dynasties, these little oysters are one of the reasons why. The ancient people fed oysters to reinforce the foundation of the bridge, perfectly integrating the architecture of the mankind and the biological traits of nature. Before you can acclaim for the wisdom and ingenuity of the ancestors, you can, in the glistening light of waves, see egrets fly by and gracefully leave, disturbing the reflections of the pavilions and pagodas in the water. With a fit of salty breath surging in your face, your train of thought will be brought back to the present.

04 泸定桥
The Luding Bridge

世界桥梁史上，泸定桥是一座开创奇迹的桥。大渡河流经泸定县时落差增大，两岸皆是三四千米的高山，使得此处河段水急浪凶，天险难逾。可此处却又是连接川藏地区的要道，古时候往来两岸竟无船可渡，只能以藤葛制索溜荡过河，凶险异常，两岸居民世代盼桥。康熙皇帝为了解决该地区交通问题，下令在此修桥。可即便中国古代桥梁修造技术享誉世界，这里复杂的水文地貌也让"浮桥""拱桥"等成熟的桥梁修造经验毫无用武之地。铁索桥成为此处唯一可能的选择。数万工匠赶赴大渡河修桥，而对岸的民众也来相助。天堑由此变坦途，而桥身的每一个铁环之上也留下了修造者的姓名。此桥一通，沟通了整个西南地区，成为连接两岸居民的纽带。

泸定桥亦是兵家必争之地，亲历了中华民族几多壮烈历史。古桥目睹了石达开的悲怆一战，也亲历了红军的勇敢顽强，在铁索游荡的几百年之间，即便两岸早已高楼林立，那些属于先人的坚韧与智慧依然回荡在大渡河上这环环相扣的铁链之间。

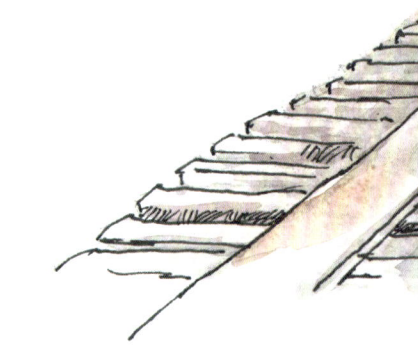

In the world's history of bridges, the Luding Bridge is the one working miracles. The drop of the Dadu River increases when it passes by Luding County. With mountains of about 3,000~4,000m high on both banks, and strong currents in this river section, it is difficult to go across. Although it is the "artery" linking Sichuan and Xizang, there was a long time when the only way to go across the river was using kudzu vine cables, which is very dangerous and risky, hence the expectation of the Xizang and Han dwellers on both banks for a bridge for generations. Emperor Kangxi issued an order to build the bridge in a bid to connect the Han and Xizang areas. Even though the bridge-building techniques of ancient China enjoyed a good fame worldwide, the mature bridge-building techniques such as "floating bridge" and "arch bridge" were not applicable to the complicated water condition and landform there. Steel cable bridge became the only possible

choice. Soon afterwards, tens of thousands of craftsmen were dispatched to the Dadu River to build the bridge with the help of the Xizang villagers across the bank. Thanks to their joint efforts, the risky "artery" became a highway and the names of the builders were imprinted on every iron hoop of the bridge body. Since it was opened to traffic, the bridge has been connecting the whole southwestern area and becomes the bond between the Han and Xizang people.

The Luding Bridge was a hotly contested spot and saw the heroic history of the Chinese nation. The ancient bridge bore witness to the sorrowful battle headed by General Shi Dakai in 1863 and the bravery and perseverance of the Red Army in 1935. After hundreds of years, modern constructions have been erected along both banks, but the tenacity and wisdom of the ancestors in architecture can still be seen through these iron chains swinging above the Dadu River.

05 赵州桥
The Zhaozhou Bridge

  隋代大匠李春建造了世界上第一座单孔敞肩石拱桥——赵州桥，它静卧于赵县的洨河之上。初时观之，世人大多被其桥身空灵、雕栏精美所吸引，却不知它曾是世界桥梁史上横空出世的"黑科技"。如长虹飞架两岸的造型引来时人惊叹，习惯了平直桥身和笨重桥墩的人们无论如何也不敢想象——桥可以没有墩。赵州桥用一弯空灵的石拱与水面的倒影形成一个美丽的玉环将两岸景致穿入环中。桥，从此不再是笨重粗直的交通工具，而成为人们心中如诗如画的美景。如诗如画的弯曲桥拱增加了桥的强度，利于泄洪，以至于在近代材料革命研发出钢筋混凝土之前，它一直是世界上最先进的桥梁建造技术。因此，经历一千四百年的洪水、地震、兵燹涂炭，世间古桥多已毁塌湮没，而赵州桥却依旧安然静卧于苍翠之中，一虹飞跨千年。

Famous master Li Chun of the Sui dynasty (581-618) built the Zhaozhou Bridge, the worldwide first single-arch stone bridge silently lying over the Jiaohe River in Zhaoxian County. At first glance, people are mostly attracted by the hollow bridge body and exquisite railings, unaware that it represents the most advanced techniques in bridge architecture of that period of time's world. The shape of a rainbow over both banks astonished the people of that time who were accustomed to straight and flat bridge bodies and heavy piers. They could not imagine that a bridge could go without piers. The hollow stone arch and its reflection in the water form a beautiful ring encompassing the scenery along the banks. The Zhaozhou Bridge is no longer a cumbersome, thick and straight construction but a poetic scene. The beautifully bent bridge arch increases the strength of the bridge structure and helps with discharging flood. It was the most advanced bridge building technique in the world before reinforced concrete was developed in the modern material revolutions. Because of this technique, the Zhaozhou Bridge is able to survive all the floods, earthquakes and wars, lying quietly in the dark green and spanning over the banks like a rainbow after thousands of years, while other ancients bridges fell into ruins.

卢沟桥
The Lugou Bridge

　　卢沟桥位于北京郊区的永定河上，是始建于金代的石质联拱桥。桥上石栏望柱间雕有数不尽的狮子，这些千姿百态、灵动喜人的石狮使得游人将"数卢沟桥上有多少狮子"成为游览必做的一桩趣事。元代来华的意大利人马可·波罗在他轰动欧洲的游记中写道："河上有一美丽石桥，各处桥梁之美鲜有及之者……它是世界上最好的，独一无二的桥。"自此，卢沟桥的美流传到西欧各国。欧洲人习惯称卢沟桥为马可·波罗桥。

　　"卢沟晓月"是著名的燕京八景之一，古时的行人常在黎明时分于古桥之上，凭栏远眺晨曦中的西山叠翠，身后未尽的月色依然皎洁妩媚。然而"卢沟桥事变"使得此桥不再仅仅作为审美对象留在人们心中，而更多地代表了中华民族勇敢抗争的精神，也使每个中国人的灵魂深处烙印下了一寸山河一寸血的民族记忆。桥上狮子无言，那或喜或悲的表情里分明是看遍了朝代更迭，亲历了家国劫难，见证了一个古老民族从历史走向新生。穿越历史的金戈铁马、硝烟战火，碧水、名桥、古城、皓月……都随古桥十七孔桥洞下的永定河水流入中华民族的记忆深处。

The Lugou Bridge over the Yongding River in the suburbs of Beijing is a stone arch bridge dating back to the Jin dynasty (1115–1234). Numerous stone lions are carved on the stone railings of the bridge. The vivid, lively stone lions of different postures make it a pleasure for the tourists to count the number of the stone lions on the Lugou Bridge. Italian explorer Marco Polo who came to China in the Yuan dynasty (1279–1368) recorded in his famous travel notes that aroused a sensation in Europe: "Over this river there is a very fine stone bridge, so fine indeed, that it has very few equals in the world." Since then, the beauty of the Lugou Bridge has been popularized to Western European countries. The Europeans are accustomed to naming the Lugou Bridge as the Marco Polo Bridge.

The Bright Moon Shining above the Lugou Bridge at Dawn is one of the eight great sights of Yanjing, now Beijing. In ancient times, the pedestrians often stood on the bridge, leaned against the railings to look into the exuberant mountains in the distance at dawn, and the bright and lovely moon high up in the sky. However, the Lugou Bridge Incident made the bridge not merely an aesthetic subject but also a symbol of the bravery and resistance of the Chinese nation. It reflects the national memory of defending the territory with hot blood existing in the depth of the soul of each Chinese. These stone lions laugh and cry in silence, almost like they feel emotions witnessing dynasty successions, nation havoc, and the great journey of an ancient nation progressing towards rebirth. The shining spears and armoured horses, the smoke of gunpowder, the blue water, the famous bridge, the ancient city and the bright moon bearing the marks of history flew into the depth of the memory of the Chinese nation like the Yongding River under the seventeen-arch ancient bridge.

07 五亭桥
The Five-Pavilion Bridge

　　五亭桥位于扬州瘦西湖内，是中国园林建筑景观桥梁的典范之作。这座清代古桥原是为了迎接乾隆皇帝驻跸江南所建，是一座风雅别致、秀丽典雅的石拱桥。所谓"五亭"是指桥面中心的五座桥亭，亭顶绿檐黄瓦，亭身红柱雕梁。四翼之亭簇拥着中心带有宝顶的高亭，各亭之间用廊相连，同气连枝，玲珑至极。桥下孔洞相互连通，于绿柳丝丝间穿洞行船，如穿画而过。亦可由洞观景，每观一洞，景辄不同，如观画数幅，中国古典园林的"借景"与"移步换景"原则在这座园林古桥身上运用得淋漓尽致，引得几百年来多少才子佳人倚楼吟眺，遥望烟树云流。五亭桥晴日虽美，但若不月夜观桥，竟也有些辜负于它。每遇皓月凌空，十五洞各衔一月，众月齐辉，金波流漾，忽闻佳人亭上吹箫……这样一场浪漫的邂逅与这座美丽绰约的古桥一样化为中国传统文化记忆深处永恒而经典的浪漫范本。

The Five-Pavilion Bridge within the Slender West Lake of Yangzhou is a quintessence of scenic bridges of Chinese gardens. Built in the Qing dynasty (1279-1911) to welcome Emperor Qianlong to Jiangnan (a region south of the Yangtze River), the ancient bridge is a graceful, handsome and exquisite stone arch bridge. The "five-pavilion" in the name refers to the five pavilions in the bridge center featuring green roofs, yellow tiles, red pillars and engraved beams. Four pavilions cluster around the highest one with a roof crown. The pavilions are exquisitely and tightly linked by verandas. The bridge arches are interconnected. Passing through these arches by boat with green willows around is like wandering in a painting. Different scenes can be seen through different bridge arches. The principles of "view borrowing" and "one step makes difference" of Chinese classical gardens can be fully reflected in the ancient bridge in the garden, attracting fine gentlemen and beautiful ladies to lean against it, chant and look afar into trees and clouds for hundreds of years. Despite the Five-Pavilion Bridge looks wonderful on sunny days, it is quite a pity not to appreciate it during the night. When the bright moon is in the sky, you can see it through any of the 15 arches. With the bright moonlight and the rippling golden waves, you can hear the pitches of a vertical bamboo flute by a young, pretty girl in the pavilion…The romantic encounter, as well as the splendid, graceful ancient bridge, become the classic quintessence of romance of the traditional Chinese culture.

08 五音桥
The Five-Pitches Bridge

河北清东陵的孝陵中顺治皇帝静静安息着，五音桥就位于顺治孝陵神道之上。顺治皇帝多愁善感、浪漫且又惆怅，他和董鄂妃的爱情故事更是荡气回肠……可能正是因为这位以爱情传奇闻名后世的皇帝带有与生俱来的浪漫气息，所以，即便是他的陵墓建筑也少有阴森之状，而是充满了浪漫的奇迹。

"五音桥"是清东陵顺治皇帝的陵区里最大、最奇特、最神秘有趣的一座七孔石桥。桥上有石制望柱、栏板、抱鼓石，尤其是一百二十六块石栏板形状和大小相同，如果用石块顺着敲击，能发出悦耳之声，清脆者悠扬，浑厚者低沉。这些声音宛若木鱼钟磬、云板筝琴，竟囊括了中国古代音乐中宫、商、角、徵、羽五音。倘徉其间，雕栏玉砌悦目竟不如五音声声悦耳，此时才惊喜地发现原来桥不仅可观、可行，竟还可听……

The remain of Emperor Shunzhi lies peacefully in the Xiaoling Tomb of the Eastern Qing Tombs in Hebei Province and the Five-Pitches Bridge erects in the Sacred Way of the Xiaoling Tomb of Emperor Shunzhi. Emperor Shunzhi was sentimental, romantic and melancholy. The love story between him and Concubine Dong'e was very touching. Maybe due to the inborn romantic of the emperor who became famous for his love story, the architecture in his tomb are not gruesome but full of romance.

The Five-Pitches Bridge is a seven-arch stone bridge of the largest, the most particular, mysterious and interesting in the tomb area of Shunzhi. There are stone balusters, balustrades and drum-shaped bearing stones on the bridge. The 126 stone balustrades are in the same shape and size. By tapping these balustrades with a stone, beautiful sounds can be heard, clear and melodious, with pitches low and deep. These sounds sound like those made by wooden knockers, bells and Chinese zithers. These sounds are in Gong, Shang, Jue, Zhi and Yu (Do, Re, Mi, Sol and La) of the ancient Chinese pitches. Walking on the bridge, you may feel that the carved balustrades and marble steps pleasant to see are no better than the five pitches pleasant to hear. Only by then can you surprisingly find that the bridge can be viewed, walked through and even heard.

09 鱼沼飞梁
Flying Bridge Across Yu Zhao

晋祠圣母殿前清泉汩汩，人们喜其泉水澄净明澈，便在此修筑鱼塘。古人向以圆者为池，方者为沼，此鱼塘为方故名"鱼沼"。鱼沼之上，一座十字形桥梁飞架其上，远处观之若大鹏展翅欲飞，遂以"鱼沼飞梁"而名。此桥东西向为正桥，连接桥两侧的献殿与圣母殿，南北向为翼桥，从正桥的桥身伸向两岸。桥边缀以白玉勾栏，可凭栏赏景。四周古柏葱茂参天，倒影映于池中。

"鱼沼飞梁"是中国古代十字形桥梁传世之孤例，同时是世界上唯一保存完整的十字形桥，也是当代立交桥的鼻祖。人在桥心凭栏俯视，如凌空而立，桥下泉水汩汩、游鱼嬉戏，瞬觉身心涤荡，洗去凡尘。若是冬季，鱼沼中泉水温热，白雾蒸腾。人置身桥上，恍如置身云端。此时心情更觉虔诚庄重，于是在走进圣母殿之前，便觉圣母的神圣威严。由是而感，"鱼沼飞梁"绝非江河之桥可比，桥的另一端通向的不是水的彼岸，而是千载昌明文化的信仰与礼制。

A clear spring gurgles in front of the Hall of Goddess of the Jin Memorial Temple. People liked the clear, limpid spring water and built a fish pond there. The ancient people would build ponds into a round shape (chi) or a square shape (zhao), so the square fish pond got its name Yu Zhao. A cross-shaped bridge was built over the fish pond, looking like Da Peng (a mythical bird of prey having enormous size and strength) flying in the distance, hence its name Flying Bridge Across Yu Zhao. The main bridge lies in the east-west direction, linking the Hall of Sacrifice and the Hall of Goddess on the banks. The minor bridge is in the south-north direction, expanding from the main bridge to the banks. The bridge edges are decorated with white jade carved balustrades against which the pedestrians can appreciate the view. Lush cypresses around the bridge erect into the sky with their reflections inverting into the pond.

Flying Bridge Across Yu Zhao is a sole example of cruciform bridges handed down from ancient China and the only intact cruciform bridge in the world, meaning it is the ancestor of the modern flyovers. Leaning upon the balustrade in the middle of the bridge is like standing on the cloud, you can see the water gurgling, the fish chasing each other, and you will feel cleansed. In winter, the spring water in the fish pond is lukewarm with mist rising above. Staying on the bridge, you may feel that you are on top of clouds and more devout than before. On the bridge, you can sense the holiness and stateliness of the Goddess even before you walk into the temple. In this respect, the Flying Bridge Across Yu Zhao can not be compared by the bridges spanning over rivers. The other end of the bridge does not only lead to the river bank but also the belief and system of rites bearing a civilized culture of thousands of years.

广济桥
The Guangji Bridge

　　广济桥位于潮州古城，始建于南宋，前后修造三百余年方成。此桥因造福一方百姓，遂以"广济百粤之民"而得名。古桥集梁桥、浮桥、拱桥于一体，是世界上最早的启闭式桥梁。广济桥浮梁结合，大桥东西两段为石梁桥，中间浮桥由十八梭船连接而成，可启可闭，此种特殊结构是我国桥梁史上的孤例。桥上样式各异、用途各别的二十四座楼台亭阁，晴日遮阳，雨季挡雨，闲时可观水景。

　　广济桥横跨韩江两岸八百余载，丰富了潮汕地区的历史人文底蕴。古老的石梁和巨大的桥墩承托着桥上传统的木构建筑，既有中国古代桥梁的共同特点，又有浓郁的潮州地方特色，是中国古桥建筑的典范之作，也是古代科学技术杰出的经典实例。古桥沿江不出数里的两岸，古老的"潮州八景"大半于此，这些充满潮州地域特色的景观与广济桥共同构成了深厚的岭南文化底蕴。

The Guangji Bridge in the ancient city of Chaozhou was initially built in the Southern Song dynasty. Its construction lasted over 300 years. The bridge was named "Guangji" (benefit all) for benefiting the people in the local area. The ancient bridge integrating the features of beam bridge, floating bridge and arch bridge is the first bridge that can open and close in the world. The Guangji Bridge has stone beams in the eastern and western sections with a floating bridge in the middle which is composed of 18 ships and can be opened and closed. It is a sole structure in the Chinese history of bridges. There are 24 elegant buildings on the bridge, each of which has a different style as well as function than others. They can be used as shelters from the sunlight and the rain, and are the perfect spots to enjoy the view.

The Guangji Bridge, which has been lying over the Hanjiang River for more than 800 years, enriches the history and the culture of the Chaoshan Region. The ancient stone beams and huge piers bear the traditional wooden structures on the bridge, displaying the shared characteristics of ancient Chinese bridges and the strong local features of Chaozhou. It is a quintessence of Chinese ancient bridges and a classic example of the outstanding science and technologies of the ancient times. More than half of the ancient Eight Sights of Chaozhou line both banks of the river which the ancient bridge spans. These sights reflecting the local characteristics of Chaozhou jointly composed the profound culture of the Lingnan Region.

第二章
Chapter 2

聚美
A Gathering Place of Beautiful Scenes

一 古镇桥群
Cluster of Ancient Bridges in Ancient Towns

绍兴古桥群
The Shaoxing Ancient Bridge Cluster

泾口桥、太平桥、接渡桥
The Jingkou Bridge, the Taiping Bridge and the Jiedu Bridge

泾口桥
The Jingkou Bridge

浙江钱塘江南岸的绍兴古城河流纵横，湖泊密布，以"东方威尼斯"之名饮誉中外。"小桥，流水，人家"是中国古人对这里最深刻的印象标签，这里以桥多且美而著称。绍兴的桥多以青石为材，其形态多姿，各具其美，小巧玲珑、优美典雅、古朴端庄、浑厚大气，每一种对桥的审美几乎都可以在绍兴找到对应物。轻盈矫健的泾口桥由三孔马蹄形拱桥与三孔石梁桥组成。这种高低错落的桥梁建筑修造布局，使整座桥梁富有流线的优美韵律和视觉的动感。桥身雕饰着生动的石狮与灵秀的莲瓣，桥身间壁又雕有文意隽永的桥联，风景、建筑、艺术与文学完美融合，构成江南水乡记忆中独特的风景。

类似的桥在绍兴还有横跨浙东运河的太平桥，它由一孔石拱桥和八孔高低不一的梁桥组成，始建于明朝。梁桥与拱桥相连，桥孔高度依次变低，最终平于水面。此地拱桥和梁桥结合的典范还有鸡笼江上的接渡桥。这座清代石桥由三孔拱桥与两孔梁桥组成，拱桥下诸孔的长宽均等，两侧梁桥延展伸出，呈现出一种对称的美感。无论四时晴阴，皆可乘一乌篷小船穿桥而过。人在船中边品绍兴黄酒，边呷茴香豆或梅菜烧肉，遥望岸边枕流而筑的古宅绣楼，闺阁少女临窗梳妆，笑语嫣然，便知江南千年以来何以如诗如画。

The ancient city of Shaoxing on the southern bank of the Qiantang River in Zhejiang is filled with rivers and lakes, thus enjoys a reputation of "Eastern Venice" at home and abroad. The poem "小桥，流水，人家 (households on both banks near a small bridge over the flowing stream)" is the deepest impression left by the ancient Chinese on the city which is famous for the numerous and gorgeous bridges there. The bridges in Shaoxing feature blue stones as the building materials. They have diverse forms and beauty; they have exquisiteness, gracefulness, simplicity and grandeur. Every kind of bridge that people like can be found in Shaoxing. The graceful but powerful Jingkou Bridge is composed of a three-arch U-shaped bridge and a three-archbeam bridge. The high-and-low bridge layout provides the bridge with beautiful rhythms and visual dynamics. The bridge body was engraved with vivid stone lions and delicately beautiful lotus petals. The separation walls of the arches were engraved with couplets of profound cultural meaning. The perfect integration of landscape, architecture, art and literature compose the unique scenery of a riverside town in the Jiangnan Ragion.

Another similar bridge in Shaoxing is the Taiping Bridge over the Zhedong Canal. Comprising a one-arch bridge and an eight-arch beam bridge of different heights, the Taiping Bridge dates back to the Ming dynasty (1368–1644). The beam bridge and the arch bridge are linked and the heights of the arches lower in sequence and finally parallel with the water surface. The Jiedu Bridge over the Jilong River is another quintessence of bridges combining arch bridges and beam bridges. This stone bridge from the Qing dynasty consists of a three-arch arch bridge and a two-arch beam bridge. The length of the arches is the same as the width. The beam bridges on both sides extend outward, developing the beauty of symmetry. Whether it is sunny or cloudy in all seasons, you can pass through the bridge in a black-awning boat. Tasting the Shaoxing rice wine and Huixiangdou (beans flavored with aniseed) or Meicai Kourou (meat with preserved vegetables) in the boat, you can appreciate the ancient houses on the bank. Then, you will know why the scenery of the riverside towns in the Jiangnan Region has been poetic and picturesque for thousands of years.

八字桥
The Bazi Bridge

　　江南水系发达的地理环境造就了江南建筑与水系之间的紧密关系，因此行走在绍兴，无论是在市井街巷还是在乡田农野，目之所及处尽是桥梁。"水港小桥多，人家尽枕河"写尽了河、桥与人之间千年的联系。此处往往是一河一街，街随河走，又或者一河两街，街以桥连。

　　八字桥位于绍兴城东南，是一座名闻遐迩的宋代古桥。它所在之地三河三路交叉相错，水陆交通汇聚于此，是古时绍兴城重要的交通枢纽。桥两端各有相对的两个落坡，从桥的任何一段望去，其形状都如"八"字，无论造型还是功能都绝似现代的立交桥。

　　古人以顺应自然的建筑理念造就了八字桥的美丽姿态和多样功能，而这种人与自然的和谐也让古桥得以长远留存，并沟通起两岸繁荣的商业、市井生活。八字桥融入了古城的文化血脉，也造就了绍兴城闻名中外的水乡社会风貌。

The advanced river system of the Yangtze River Delta breeds a close tie between the architecture and the river system there. Therefore, walking in the street or field in Shaoxing, you can see bridges everywhere. The verse "there are many bridges in the port and the people there live at the riverside" depicts the connections between rivers, bridges and people. In Shaoxing, when there is a river, there is a street along it. Sometimes there are two streets along the river with a bridge connecting them.

The Bazi Bridge in the southeast of Shaoxing is a widely-known ancient bridge built in the Song dynasty. At the intersection of three rivers and three roads, and with land and water communication gathering there, it was a pivotal hub of communication in ancient Shaoxing. There are two slopes opposite to each other on both ends of the bridge, looking like the Chinese character "丿\" when they are seen at any section of the bridge and resembling the modern overpasses in terms of modeling and function.

With the architectural concept of living in harmony with nature, the ancients created the magnificent posture and diverse functions of the Bazi Bridge and such harmony enabled the ancient bridge to be kept, benefiting the prosperous commercial and ordinary life on both banks. The Bazi Bridge becomes a part of the culture of the ancient city and fosters the social landscape of the region of rivers in Shaoxing known at home and abroad.

纤道桥
The Qiandao Bridge

绍兴作为水乡城市，自然是离不开船的。这里的乌篷船如同威尼斯的贡多拉一样古今闻名。水多船密的拥挤河道中，纤夫自然是不可少的，纤道桥便由此得名。纤道桥始建于唐，桥墩、桥面俱以条石拼成，桥长而孔多，桥身贴近水面，与河流平行便于纤夫拉纤。每遇疾风险浪，船也可通过桥孔进入浅水区躲避风浪，故纤道桥有"避塘"之称。因此桥的重要性、公益性，历代多为政府出资修建，故亦有"官塘"之称。千百年来，水乡居民早已将"百孔官塘"当作了水乡胜景，此处不仅供纤夫拉纤之用，也是通往集镇的交通要道。春和晴日，舟行水上，桥如白玉长堤，放眼望去纤夫奋力拉纤，桥上行人往来，船中乘客安坐，此种水乡景观绵延数十里，联结了人、水、船、桥，将水乡元素尽收眼底，方才了然水乡亦桥乡。

As a riverside city, Shaoxing boasts numerous boats. The black-awning boats are as famous as the Gondolas in Venice. Boat trackers are indispensable in the watercourse densely crowded with boats, who use the bridge as a track road, hence the name Qiandao, which means towpath in Chinese. The Qiandao Bridge was initially built in the Tang dynasty (618–907). The piers and bridge surface were made of stone strips. The bridge is long and has many arches, with its body close to the water surface, parallel with the river to make it convenient for the road trackers to work. Boats can go through the arches and enter the shallows to elude stormy waves, so the Qiandao Bridge is also called "Wave-Eluding Pond." Because of its importance and public benefit, the bridge was built and repaired with government finance of different dynasties and therefore got the name "government pond." For thousands of years, the riverside citizens have taken the "100-arch government pond" as wonderful riverside scenery. It is used not merely by the boat trackers but also as the vital communication line to towns. Riding a boat on sunny spring days, you can see the bridge looking like a white jade dyke, boat trackers arduously towing boats, passers-by coming and going on the bridge and passengers sitting peacefully in the boats. Looking at the riverside landscape stretching into the distance, you can have a panoramic view of the elements of the region of rivers consisting of people, water, boats and bridges and know that the region of rivers is also the town of bridges.

广宁桥
The Guangning Bridge

广宁桥据传始建于南宋之前,是中国现存最长的七折边拱单孔古桥。广宁桥中心正对着绍兴城的大善塔,在桥上又可见绍兴城南诸山,于是自南宋以来,广宁桥一直是绍兴城绝佳观景之处。广宁桥与八字桥相去不甚远,虽同是古老的立交桥,但疏导交通的功能却大不相同,广宁桥的桥拱下设有纤道,可供纤夫通行。广宁桥所在之处,古时是绍兴城内重要的运河码头,这一河段早在唐代已十分繁忙,众多纤夫往来于河道两边的纤道之上,不必上岸绕行,十分方便。广宁桥对立体交通的空间关系处理反映着古人与自然对话的方式,也使这座古代桥梁充满了亲水的元素和鲜明的水乡特征。

广宁桥的桥栏柱雄健厚实,雕刻遍饰,精美典雅,举目远山叠翠茂盛,桥下乌篷船争流。桥旁成片的青砖黛瓦、市井人家,行走其间耳边尽是吴侬软语。明清古宅依旧,朱漆窗牖、木雕楹柱,与街边河上拱桥、乌船融为一体,几百年来悠然安坐于烟火人间。

The Guangning Bridge said to be built before the Southern Song dynasty is the longest seven-zigzag single-archancient bridge existing in China. The center of the Guangning Bridge is opposite to the Dashan Tower in Shaoxing. On the bridge, you can also see the mountains in the southern part of Shaoxing. For this reason, the Guangning Bridge has been an ideal site to enjoy the view of Shaoxing since the Southern Song dynasty. The Guangning Bridge and the Bazi Bridge are not far away from each other. Although they are both ancient overpasses, their ways of dispersing traffic are quite different. Towpaths were set under the arches of the Guangning Bridge for the passage of boat trackers. Near the location of the Guangning Bridge was an important wharf in ancient Shaoxing. This river section was busy since the Tang dynasty. Numerous boat trackers conveniently came to and fro the towpaths on both banks of the watercourse and didn't need to go ashore and detour. The spatial relationship of the Guangning Bridge with three-dimensional transportation can reflect the attitude of the ancients to nature and endow the ancient bridge with waterside elements and distinctive features of waterside regions.

The Guangning Bridge features thick and solid balusters with exquisitely decorative carvings. You can see those exuberant green mountains in the distance, black-awning boats under the bridge, stretches of black bricks and tiles and households beside the bridge. Walking nearby, you can hear the soft Suzhou dialect. The ancient houses of the Ming and Qing dynasty, featuring red-painted wooden windows, wooden columns and pillars, integrating with the arch bridge and the black-awning boats on the river nearby the streets, still look the same as before, leisurely sitting in the world of mortals for centuries.

05 题扇桥、拜王桥
The Tishan Bridge and the Baiwang Bridge

题扇桥
The Tishan Bridge

江南千年富庶繁盛，其文化充满诗性，绍兴的水与桥、人与物以其深广的人文意蕴深刻地影响了中国文化与审美。在这种诗性且美好的文化环境中，才俊辈出；而绍兴的桥，也不乏与才子名士、帝王将相结缘的传奇掌故。

位于古城蕺山街上的题扇桥，相传一代书圣王羲之曾在此居住。他每出宅第途经蕺山街便会过此桥，一日桥上遇卖扇老妪，因怜其生计艰难，便在老妪所卖之扇上题字，助其售卖，所题之扇往往被高价抢购一空。于是这座古桥，遂以"题扇桥"为名。桥旁尚有插天灯的柱础遗迹。古时，桥旁天灯散发出昏黄的灯光，为晚归行人照亮归途，也为夜航船中的人们指明航向。

隐蔽在居民里弄间的拜王桥则是一座大隐隐于市的唐代五折单孔石拱桥，旧传吴越武肃王平董昌之乱后，郡人拜谒于此，桥故以"拜王"为名。从桥上望去，一眼就可见越王台残破斑驳的城墙，悠然凄怆之感油然而生。

　　这些桥带着各自的故事在水一方，创造了"三山万户巷盘曲，百桥千街水纵横"的淡雅灵秀与水乡文化。若乘乌篷船沿河道游弋其间，无论是烟火气息的杂居里弄，还是清雅端严的大夫宅第，都在流金岁月的光影间逐渐漫漶，带着满是水乡泽国厚重的文化底蕴与诗性的光辉，待人探寻。

The Jiangnan Region has always been prosperous and culturally poetic. The water, bridges, people and materials of Shaoxing have profoundly influenced the Chinese culture and aesthetics with their deep and extensive cultural deposits. The poetic and excellent cultural environment bred generations of talents there. The bridges in Shaoxing boast legends and anecdotes about talents, celebrities, emperors, generals and ministers.

　　The Tishan Bridge is on the Jishan Street of the ancient city where it is said the former residence of eminent calligrapher Wang Xizhi was. He would go through the bridge whenever he went past the Jishan Street. One day, he met an old woman selling fans on the bridge. Sympathized with her hard life, he wrote on the fans she sold to help her. Those fans were sold out at a high price very quickly. Therefore the bridge got the name Tishan, which means write on fans in Chinese. The trace of plinth where the sky lanterns were inserted remains near the bridge. In ancient times, the sky lanterns gave out dim light near the bridge, lighting up the homeward journey for the pedestrians returning home late and pointing out the course for the people boating at night.

　　The Baiwang Bridge hidden in the alley is a five-zigzag single-arch stone bridge built in the Tang dynasty. Legend has it that the residents paid their respects to King Wusu of the Wuyue Kingdom there after he resolving an insurrection in this place. Therefore, the bridge was named Baiwang Bridge, which in Chinese means the bridge of respecting the king. Looking into the distance on the bridge, you can see the dilapidated, mottled walls of the Platform of the King of Yue, with the sense of misery welling up in the heart.

　　These bridges, along with their own unforgettable stories, create the quiet, elegant and beautiful scenery as well as waterside culture, just like the poem describes: "there are three mountains, hundreds of thousands of households, and tortuous alleys; There are hundreds of bridges, thousands of streets, and crossing rivers." When you take a black-awning boat along the river, you will experience the elapse of time in the streets and lanes of the mortals or in the solemn mansions of the ministers. The profound culture and poetic glory of the waterside area await exploration by others from the outside world.

光相桥、谢公桥
The Guangxiang Bridge and the Xiegong Bridge

绍兴的桥跨越千年,不仅联结着江南水岸,也联结着世俗与宗教。光相桥位于绍兴古城西北,因桥畔原有光相寺而得名。该桥为单跨半圆形石拱桥,因其为世俗信众必须过此桥才能进寺上香朝拜,所以桥身拱石尽是莲花须弥座图案,并刻有"南无阿弥陀佛"等字。"光相"原意指此处舍利子光芒灿烂,于是光相桥便在古寺的佛殿香火、梵音朗朗中屹立不倒,即便后来光相寺与舍利子已无存,但古桥依旧悄然立于河上,石阶与拱石的缝隙间新生的绿色见证着一个个寒暑春秋。

谢公桥为单孔七折石拱桥,始建于后晋。据宋代方志记述,此桥的"谢公"乃是指谢灵运。桥名虽不见梵意,但每一块拱石上都刻有莲花须弥座图案,刻字中捐款人姓名多有"信士"字样,可见此桥是由佛教信众捐建而成的。它显示了佛教如何在点滴之间影响着世俗世界的社会生活,将佛经中的圆融智慧播撒进乡间里弄及深宅大院之中。于清晨微风渐起时行走在临水街岸,于落日余晖时静坐在乌篷船中,或可感念早已消失的晨钟暮鼓、青灯古佛。

The bridges in Shaoxing have a history of more than 1,000 years, linking not merely the river banks in the Jiangnan Region but also the mortal world and religion. The Guangxiang Bridge in the northwestern part of the ancient city of Shaoxing got its name because of the previous Guangxiang Temple on the bank. It is a single-span semicircular stone arch bridge. Since the mortal believers must go through it to the temple to pray and worship their gods, the bridge body and the stone arches feature the design of Sumeru seat and lotus seat, and the Chinese translation of Amitābha. The name Guangxiang refers to the brilliance of Śarīra. The Guangxiang Bridge erects firmly amid the incense and Sanskrit, even though the Guangxiang Temple and Śarīra are long gone, the ancient bridge still spans over the river. The green in the cracks of the bridge body have witnessed countless seasons there.

The Xiegong Bridge is a single-arch seven-zigzag stone bridge initially built in the later Jin dynasty (936-947). According to the local chronicle of the Song dynasty, "Xiegong" (Duke Xie) here refers to Xie Lingyun, a poet of the Southern and Northern Dynasties. Although the name of the bridge has no connection with Buddhism, each arch stone is engraved with a Sumeru seat or a lotus seat. Since the name of the donors inscribed on the bridge body includes the Chinese characters meaning "believer," it can be thus seen that the bridge was built with the donation of Buddhist believers. It depicts how Buddhism influences the social life of the mortal world and spreads the wisdom in the Buddhist texts into the rural lanes and courtyards. You can walk on the riverside banks amid the breeze at dawn, sit quietly in a black awning boat in the sunset, maybe you will be able to hear the morning bells and evening drums as well as seeing the oil lamps before the statues of the Buddha that have been long gone.

光相桥
The Guangxiang Bridge

07 泗龙桥
The Silong Bridge

　　泗龙桥坐落于绍兴的鉴湖之上，始建于宋朝，据传此桥前身是中国古代诗歌中多次被题咏的鲁墟桥。这座古桥由三孔联拱桥与二十孔石梁桥组成。此桥宛若一条曲颈卧水的长龙横跨鉴湖，气势宏伟，景观秀美。宋代诗人陆游曾感叹过："千金不须买画图，听我长歌歌鉴湖。"可见千载之前的古人已经深深为鉴湖的景致所陶醉，而在这美景之中必不可少泗龙桥的点缀。多孔的拱桥和平直的梁桥在宽阔水面的结合，使泗龙桥的建筑形式更加多元，姿态更加优美。而古桥的功能也因为这种多元的建筑形式变得丰富起来，高耸的桥拱可以方便往来船只过河，但若全桥皆用这种高耸的拱桥形式，则会让往来行人过桥如翻山越岭，颇感疲累。于是一段平直的梁桥可以让行人步履轻松，再过一段拱桥亦不觉累，在拱桥之顶望桥下往来船只也更觉兴致盎然。人与船各行其道，人与水亲和互惠，充分彰显了中国传统桥梁建筑的生态价值。

　　The Silong Bridge sitting on the Jianhu Lake in Shaoxing was initially built in the Song dynasty. It is said that its predecessor is the Luxu Bridge repeatedly mentioned in ancient Chinese poems. The ancient bridge consists of a three-arch arch bridge and a twenty-arch stone beam bridge. Spanning over the Jianhu Lake like a long dragon with its neck dipping into the river, the bridge is famous for its imposing grandeur and splendid scenery. Poet Lu You of the Song dynasty once said: "There is no need to spend much on a picture. You can just

listen to my poem in praise of the Jianhu Lake." Thus It can be seen that the ancients were deeply enchanted by the scenery of the Jianhu Lake with the indispensable decoration of the Silong Bridge. The combination of the multi-arch arch bridge and the straight beam bridge on the vast river surface diversifies the architectural forms and beautifies the postures of the Silong Bridge. The functions of the ancient bridge are improved with the diverse architectural forms. The towering bridge arches facilitated the passage of the vessels. However, if the whole bridge had adopted these lofty arches, the passers-by would feel it tiring to walk on the bridge as if they were climbing mountains. On the other hand, a straight beam bridge can make the pedestrians walk easily and without tiredness even after going over an arch, not spoiling the fun of overlooking the vessels from the arch bridge. There are different ways for pedestrians and boats. The pedestrians and the water are in affinity and reciprocity, fully manifesting the value of traditional Chinese bridges.

故宫金水桥
The Golden Water Bridges in the Palace Museum

01 外金水桥
The Outer Golden Water Bridge

金水桥群位于北京天安门区域。外金水桥位于天安门、太庙、中山公园前,横亘在天安门广场和天安门城楼之间,原是由七座三孔拱桥组成的桥群。古时文武百官便是通过这里进入代表权力巅峰的紫禁城。

金水桥桥身微拱,似"蹑玉桥之长虹",使桥面形成一个极为缓的坡度,从桥上走向紫禁城时,人的视线汇聚于天安门城楼下的深邃入口,敬畏之感油然而生。这组桥群彰显了君主至高无上的权力,每一座桥的装饰细节和使用规则都将等级和权力体现得淋漓尽致。君王、贵族、平民过此桥时各行其道,居中的那座最华丽的雕刻着龙的桥仅供帝王通行。

光阴荏苒,几百年间,金水桥身后的紫禁城中朝代更迭,皇位与权力几番易手后终随时代而远去。如今的金水桥不再代表帝王荣耀与特权,但古桥那端庄整肃的身影始终是中国文化与记忆中一个永恒的焦点,川流不息的游人总是行至于此停下脚步反复回眸。

The Golden Water Bridge cluster lies in the area of the Tian'anmen Square, Beijing. The Outer Golden Water Bridge in front of the Tian'anmen, the Imperial Ancestral Temple and the Zhongshan Park and separating the Tian'anmen Square and the Tian'anmen Gate tower was originally a bridge cluster consisting of seven three-arch arch bridges. In ancient times, civil and military officials entered the Forbidden City representing the supreme power through there.

The body of the Golden Water Bridge is a small arch like a long rainbow making the bridge surface form a gentle slope. When you walk through the bridge into the Forbidden City, your sight focuses on the deep entrance below the Tian'anmen Gate tower, feeling a sense of reverence arising spontaneously. The bridge cluster fully manifests the supreme power of the emperors, and the division of classes and power through details of decoration and rules of use of each bridge. The emperors, nobles and civilians should go through the bridge cluster by different bridges. The most magnificent bridge with engraved dragons in the center was dedicated to the use of the emperors.

Time passes very quickly. During centuries, the Forbidden City behind the Golden Water Bridge saw a succession of different dynasties. The throne and imperial power were finally lost in the end. The present Golden Water Bridge no longer represents the glory and privilege of the emperors, but the dignified and solemn ancient bridge is the permanent focus of the Chinese culture and national memory where the tourists in streams often stop their steps and look back.

02 内金水桥
The Inner Golden Water Bridge

几百年前，德国古典哲学家康德提出了审美的重要标准——优美与崇高。而恰在同一历史时期的中国，一组皇家古桥却将这种优美与崇高融于一体，造物于世间。

故宫的午门与太和门之间，坐落着五座石桥，这便是内金水桥。桥下的人工河道，是在修建紫禁城时，古代帝王按照中国传统的风水原则布局的。五座白玉桥的装饰极尽奢华，桥上望柱和栏板皆以白玉精雕，正对着通向终极权力入口的太和门。蓝天白云下，举目皆是皇宫的红墙黄瓦。在这个封闭的宽阔空间中，远处高大庄严的台阶丹墀与坡缓起伏的古桥遥遥相对。古桥群舒缓优美的造型，更能衬托出周围建筑群的无上威严。

人们行步桥上，随着桥面的起伏不但能感受到君王至高权力，也能陶醉于古典建筑的优美之中。此刻，"美与崇高"再不是书本上枯燥难懂的文字，而成为震撼心灵、跨越东西方文化的共同感受。

Centuries ago, German classical philosopher Kant proposed an important criterion of aesthetics—beauty and sublimity. In China and in the same period, a group of imperial ancient bridges successfully integrated the beauty and sublimity.

Five stone bridges erecting between the Meridian Gate and the Gate of Supreme Harmony of the Palace Museum compose the Inner Golden Water Bridge cluster. The man-made watercourse under the bridge was laid out according to the traditional Chinese geomancy as required by ancient emperors while building the Forbidden City. The decoration of the five alabaster bridges is extremely luxurious. The balusters and the balustrades of the bridges are exquisitely engraved with alabaster, just opposite to the entrance to the supreme

power—the Gate of Supreme Harmony. What a good sight with red walls and yellow tiles of the imperial palace against the backdrop of blue sky and white clouds! In the closed, broad space, the tall and solemn red steps leading up to the imperial palace are distantly opposite to the ancient bridges with rolling slopes. The graceful shape of the ancient bridge cluster can set off the supreme stateliness of the surrounding architectures.

Walking on the pedestrian bridge, you can not only experience the supreme power of the emperors but get intoxicated in the beauty of classical architectures with the rolling bridge surface. At that moment, "beauty and sublimity" are no longer boring, elusive words in textbooks but shared feelings stirring the heart and bridging the Eastern and Western culture.

德清古桥群
The Deqing Ancient Bridge Cluster

01 寿昌桥、永安桥
The Shouchang Bridge and the Yong'an Bridge

宋代以来，随着中国经济重心由北向南发展，江南地区的繁荣富庶渐超前朝。南宋时期，皇权中心南迁，中国文化与历史自此多了一份由水乡氤氲之气带来的澄明与温柔。桥便是水乡江南文化中醒目的标志。

德清县地处浙江省北部，古时是金陵至杭州的古道要津，故而风物与名胜多始建于宋。寿昌桥即是宋代所建，所用石材是当地一种独有的武康石，德清许多古桥亦是选用此石。寿昌桥虽然是单孔石桥，桥面却不似其他单孔桥那样陡，悠长坡缓的桥面可让人闲游信步。遥望古桥，曲线柔和，气韵清雅，斑驳的桥身爬满碧翠的藤蔓，桥面微拱的弧线、桥拱与水面倒影相拼而成的圆环，都与远山起伏的线条相映成趣，演绎着水乡小城中充满乡愁的江南意境。德清县内，还有一座同为宋代单孔古桥的永安桥，形制颇似寿昌桥。桥上莲花望柱、桥身漫卷云纹虽经岁月漫漶，却依稀可辨大宋之风雅逸趣，与河两岸的小镇居民世代演绎着"小桥流水人家"的市井生活。

With the shift of China's economic center from the north to the south, the prosperity of the Jiangnan Region surpassed that before. In the Southern Song dynasty, the center of imperial power and authority shifted southward. The Chinese culture and history were endowed with the clarity and gentleness brought by the region of rivers. The bridges are the conspicuous symbol of the culture of this region.

Deqing County located in northern Zhejiang was a key post on the ancient path from Nanjing to Hangzhou in ancient times. Therefore, the scenery and scenic spots there were mostly started building in the Song dynasty. The Shouchang Bridge was built in the Song dynasty with Wukang stones native to the local area. Many ancient bridges in Deqing County were built with such stones. Although the Shouchang Bridge is a single-arch stone bridge, the bridge surface is not as steep as that of other single-arch bridges and makes it possible for pedestrians to walk leisurely on the slight slopes. Looking at the ancient bridge in the distance, you can see its gentle lines, artistic elegance, green vines all over the mottled bridge body, the slight arc of the bridge surface and the ring made by the bridge arch and its reflection in the water form a delightful contrast with the undulating lines of remote mountains, displaying the nostalgic perception of the riverside towns in the Jiangnan Region. The Yong'an Bridge is a single-arch bridge built in the Song dynasty resembling the Shouchang Bridge in Deqing County. The lotus balusters on the bridge and the cirrus cloud pattern of the bridge body can still manifest the elegant style and mien of the Song dynasty despite the erosion over years and accompany the residents along the river to live the ordinary life describing in the verse "households on both banks near a small bridge over the flowing stream" for generations.

寿昌桥
The Shouchang Bridge

万寿桥
The Wanshou Bridge

　　万寿桥又名万善桥，是一座单孔石拱桥，桥身多饰乳丁纹，桥上有莲花望柱，此种外形与修造技术与宋桥如出一辙，因此，这座古桥虽始建于元代，但在桥梁修造技术上上承宋制。

　　桥顶券面石上有篆书"万寿"两字，桥拱用条石纵联砌成，如一道卧虹沉睡在古镇中。如其他那些散落在田野乡间的江南古桥一样，万寿桥虽历经风雨摧折，桥身斑驳，石雕漫漶，但桥体藤蔓遍布，绿意盎然，桥拱和水中倒影合璧，如穿水碧玉环，将烟雨江南的钟灵毓秀收于碧玉环中供观赏，给水乡濡染几分灵性，为儒生滋长一点慧根。如今，那些依稀的宋元往事，已随江南的霏霏细雨而逐渐湮灭，唯有这些古桥无言坚守，守护着游子心中永恒的乡愁。

    The Wanshou Bridge, also called Wanshan Bridge, is a single-arch stone bridge featuring stone dots over the bridge body and lotus balusters on the bridge. The appearance and building techniques are like those of the bridges of the Song dynasty despite that this ancient bridge was built in the Yuan dynasty.

    The two characters 万寿 (Wanshou, meaning longevity) were carved in seal script on the stone of the bridge top and the arches were built with stone strips like a rainbow over the ancient town. Like other ancient bridges scattering in the fields of the Jiangnan Region, despite the mottled bridge bodies and the vague stone carvings due to the weathering, the bridge still features green vines all over. The arches and the reflection in the river, together like a jade ring in the water, show the unique beauty of the mist-shrouded riverside towns in the Jiangnan Region and add some characteristics to the scenery of the riverside area and the root of wisdom to the Confucian scholars. Now, the vague events of the Song and Yuan dynasties have vanished in the light rain, only leaving the ancient bridges to safeguard the permanent nostalgia lingering in the mind of the wanderers far away from home.

普济桥
The Puji Bridge

德清县所在的湖州是千古名城,"云溪""乌程"这些唐诗宋词中耳熟能详的地名,早已刻印在中国人的文化记忆中。明嘉靖时期《德清县志》记载此处云:"居泽国间,水利其舟……乃若舍舟遵陆,非桥渡通。"这种独特的地理环境孕育了富于江浙特色的德清古桥群,也诞生了许多和桥息息相关的风土人情。

普济桥始建于宋,是一座三孔梁桥。它位于蠡山村,据传是范蠡和西施的隐居地。从古至今,此段水路两岸居民甚多,许多千年古桥已经无法承载今日熙来攘往的行人车辆。于是那些古今路人印象里建造精良、外形秀雅的古桥一座座无声无息地消失在我们的视觉和记忆中,待到人们惊觉时,此处水段便只剩下了普济桥。闲时立于桥畔,凝视河面波光,时光宛若凝固,忽来清风吹皱河水。见水中倒影,于阳光下浮想联翩——范蠡、西施可有驻足于此同观涟漪?

Huzhou, to which Deqing County belongs, is a famous city with a long history. The place names such as Yunxi and Wucheng familiar in Chinese poetry have long been imprinted in the cultural memory of the Chinese people. It is recorded in the *Town Record of Deqing* composed in the Ming dynasty: "The rivers in Deqing make it a land of boats. It is necessary to go through the bridge to get off the boats and onto the land." The unique geological environment breed the unique ancient bridge clusters of Jiangsu and Zhejiang as well as the local customs and practices relating to bridges.

The Puji Bridge dating back to the Song dynasty is a three-arch beam bridge located in Lishan Village which is said to be the secluded place of Fan Li and Xi Shi[1]. Since ancient times, there have been numerous residents on both banks of the waterway. Many millennia-old ancient bridges can not bear the weight of the busy traffic. Therefore, the exquisitely built and apparently elegant ancient bridges in the mind of the passersby in ancient times have quietly disappeared from our sight and memory. When people finally notice it, only the Puji Bridge is still existed in this water section. Standing on the side of the bridge at leisure and looking fixedly at the sparkling light of waves on the river surface, you will feel like time is still as if it was frozen. Suddenly, clear wind troubles the river surface. You can see the reflections in the water and fall into a reverie under the sun—have Fan Li and Xi Shi once stayed here and appreciated the ripples together?

---

1 Fan Li and Xi Shi are famous figures of the Spring and Autumn Period of China. Fan is an excellent politician and strategist with big influence, and Xi, as Fan's lover, is said to be one of the most beautiful women in history.

04 社桥、青云桥、兼济桥
The Sheqiao Bridge, the Qingyun Bridge and the Jianji Bridge

　　南宋时期，朝廷南渡，让本已富裕繁华的江南在文化艺术与科学技术方面有了进一步的发展。水网密布，枕河而居，沿河设街的独特地理环境使得江南地区出现了一个桥梁修造的巅峰期，其修造之高妙，雕饰之精美令后世桥梁无法与之媲美。

　　武康镇盛产的武康石是江南古桥最重要的建筑材料。社桥造型简洁凌空高挑，一派风雅宋意，是武康石作为建桥材料的典范之作。桥身望柱以简约素雅的莲瓣雕刻装饰，桥身的宋元构件犹存。雷甸村的青云桥坡缓桥长，古朴悠然。而此地的兼济桥更是胸怀"兼济天下"的社会责任感，使附近百姓咸与受益。这几百年间的修造，终于形成出门见桥、舟泊桥边的生活习惯与人文景观。在晴日中赏碧波卧虹，于雪后品古桥残雪。在历史与岁月的流逝中，许多古桥慢慢隐去了身影，后人只能从这些尚存世的古桥中，一窥古人风雅、高洁的艺术审美和对胸怀天下、惠济众生的美好向往。

青云桥
the Qingyun Bridge

社桥
The Sheqiao Bridge

    The imperial court moved southward in the Southern Song dynasty, pushing ahead the development of the originally prosperous Jiangnan Region in culture, art, science and technology. People there lived in an area densely covered with water networks and built the streets along the rivers. The unique geological environment brought bridge construction to a peak. The masterly bridge building techniques and the exquisite embellishments made future bridges incomparable.

    Wukang stones produced in Wukang Town are the most important materials for building ancient bridges in the Jiangnan Region. The Sheqiao Bridge featuring a simple shape, towering aloft and showing the gracefulness of the Song dynasty is a quintessence of using Wukang stones as bridge building materials. The balusters on the bridge are decorated with engraved plain and elegant lotus and the components of the Song and Yuan dynasties still exist. The Qingyun Bridge in Leidian Village of primitive simplicity features a slight slope and a long body. The Jianji Bridge implying cherishing the sense of social responsibility benefited the people nearby. The construction of bridges over centuries developed people's living habit as well as a culture scene of traveling by boat and berthing boats by the bridges. You can appreciate the waves and rainbows on sunny days and residual snow on the ancient bridge. In the elapse of years, many ancient bridges have gradually faded out and the future generations can only glance at the ancestors' elegant style, lofty artistic aesthetics and eager yearning to shoulder social responsibilities and benefit the people through the existing ancient bridges.

沘江古桥群
The Bijiang River Ancient Bridge Cluster

01 青云桥
The Qingyun Bridge

青云桥地处滇西澜沧江畔的云龙县，这里不仅是风景旖旎的秀丽之地，也是古代茶马古道的必经之所。山峦密布、水网纵横，几百年间马帮商队熙熙攘攘，桥在这里，不只是交通工具，更关乎无数人一辈子的生计与希望。

青云桥是一座架设在沘江两岸山壁之间的铁链吊桥，桥底有五条铁链，其上铺置木板组成桥面，左右两边各有一条作为扶手的铁链，东西两端建有桥亭，亭中雕有文采斐然的造桥题记、精美静谧的佛像。此地古时因产盐而富，耕樵之家子弟也因此有机会读书识字，走出大山后甚至成为执掌一方权柄的封疆大吏。他们归乡省亲追忆慈母时，发现家乡父老越江过河依然艰险，便捐资造桥，以造福乡梓。此后，那些游子淡淡的乡愁中便总是藏着一座幼时记忆的桥，而母亲的慈祥身影总在桥边翘首盼归。手扶铁链，耳闻桥下浊浪涛声，身旁驮畜载着两岸货物缓缓而过，人与时光仿佛都在古桥的悠然有序的晃动间慢慢凝滞。

The Qingyun Bridge is in Yunlong County, which is on the bank of Lancang River in western Yunnan and is not just a beautiful land of charming scenery but was also an important town of the ancient Tea Horse Road. Surrounded by dense mountains and water networks, the bridge witnessed the bustling trade caravans over centuries. The bridge there is not merely a means of communication but also concerns people's livelihood and hopes.

The Qingyun Bridge, a chain bridge linking the two mountains of the Bijiang River, has five iron chains beneath the bridge, a surface paved with planks and an iron chain on either side as balustrade. There is a pavilion on the eastern and western ends of the bridge respectively, housing gorgeous engraved inscriptions as well as fine and solemn Buddhist statues. Yunlong County became rich as a source of salt in ancient times. Even a child of a laborer had the chance of learning and becoming a powerful official. When he returned to his hometown to mourn for his mother, he found that people there still had to cross the river riskily. So he donated to build this bridge to benefit his hometown. Afterwards, the bridge is often the image in the dim nostalgia of the wanderers far away from home, with the figures of their kind mothers standing by the bridge and expecting their return in their childhood. Standing by the iron chains, you can hear the torrential waves under the bridge, while pack animals passing by with heavy loads. People and time seem to freeze slowly in the orderly sway of the ancient bridge.

02 中州桥
The Zhongzhou Bridge

　　云南山多、水多，自然桥也多。这里复杂的地貌、多元的民族构成使这些古桥结构各异、式样繁多，名闻遐迩者有之，默默无闻者亦有之。澜沧江与沘江组成了纵横交错的水网，那里有一个叫果郎村的小村子，当地居民为征服自然，便在湍急的河流和陡峭的山谷间，建造了一座铁索吊桥——中州桥。

　　清中期，中州桥为一墩二孔的木梁廊桥，因为这是茶马古道西去的第一座桥，马帮驮队的重载，风雨雷暴的摧残，终使桥身残破，附近居民便将桥改建成更适合当地环境的铁索吊桥。桥面上横竖相抵的木板至今仍承载着滇西最后的马帮商队驮运着沉沉的货物缓缓而过。清脆的马蹄声声，浓浓的普洱茶香，洁白的盐田井盐……几百年间，无数马帮商队就是这样跨过了一座座看似平凡却又古老的桥。桥，在沉默中见证了历史，融入了当地居民的生活，而人们也默默守护着古桥，守护着他们世代相传的质朴生活。

Yunnan, boasting plenty of mountains and rivers, is also a land of bridges. The complicated landforms and diverse ethnic groups generate diverse styles and patterns of these ancient bridges. Some of them are widely known while others are not. The Lancang River and the Bijiang River form a criss-crossed water network. There is a small village called Guolang Village. To conquer nature, the local villagers built an iron chain suspension bridge, namely, the Zhongzhou Bridge, above the torrential river and across the steep valley.

In the mid-Qing dynasty, the Zhongzhou Bridge was a beam veranda bridge with one pier and two arches. It was the first bridge leading westward of the Ancient Tea Horse Road. The heavy load of the caravan and the damages by wind, rain, thunder and storm resulted in the dilapidation of the bridge body. The villagers nearby rebuilt the bridge into an iron chain suspension bridge more suitable for the local environment. The crossing planks on the bridge surface carries the heavy goods of the last caravans in western Yunnan passing by slowly. The loud sounds of hoofs, the strong fragrance of Pu'er tea, the white well salt... For centuries, numerous caravans crossed these seemingly ordinary and old bridges. The bridge witnesses the history in silence and gets integrated into the local life. People there silently safeguard the ancient bridge and the simple life there for generations.

03 安澜桥、阳春桥、永镇桥
The Anlan Bridge, the Yangchun Bridge and the Yongzhen Bridge

　　千百年来，多个民族生活耕作在滇西云龙县，奔流的沘江波浪声声，成为了本地居民生活中的一部分。这里多元的文化造就了种类齐全、风格多样的众多古桥，故有"世界古桥梁艺术博物馆"的美誉。

　　"长春三渡"这个诗一般的名字代表了沘江上的三座清代古桥——安澜桥、阳春桥、永镇桥。安澜桥是清乾隆年间始建的铁链吊桥，桥身铁链铺木板而成，简朴实用。东边不远处有另外两座清代木制廊桥：阳春桥、永镇桥。阳春桥桥身斑驳沧桑，饱经岁月风雨的冲刷，至今仍坚强屹立的小桥亭和桥廊，为往来乡民撑起一片遮风挡雨的小天地。永镇桥状若马鞍，卧虹般悬于河上，弧度优美。这些古桥远离闹市安卧古城，几百年来默默地注视着桥上往来的乡民、嬉闹喧哗的孩童，也会悄悄掩藏着小情侣桥亭中的密语，每日伫立无言中记载着时间的沧桑，流转着人间烟火的温暖。

永镇桥
Yongzhen Bridge

For thousands of years, people of different ethnic groups have lived and plowed in Yunlong County, western Yunnan. The sounds of the rushing Bijiang River became part of the local life. The diverse culture gave rise to multitudes of ancient bridges of all sorts, styles and patterns. It got the fame as the "World's Ancient Bridge Art Museum."

There are three ancient bridges built in the Qing dynasty over the Bijiang River, namely, the Anlan Bridge, the Yangchun Bridge and the Yongzhen Bridge. The plain, practical Anlan Bridge, an iron chain suspension bridge built in the reign of Emperor Qianlong of the Qing dynasty, is made with planks connected with iron chains. Two wooden veranda bridges, namely, the Yangchun Bridge and the Yongzhen Bridge, which were built in the Qing dynasty, are located nearby to the east. The Yangchun Bridge is mottled all over and brushed by wind and rain over years. The bridge pavilion and veranda staying strong today offer shelter for the citizens there. In the shape of a saddle, the Yongzhen Bridge spans over the river with a graceful radian. The ancient bridges far away from the noise and lying in the ancient city have been watching the residents coming to and fro, the children frolicking on the bridge and couples whispering in the pavilion. Recording the vicissitudes of time silently every day, they carry the warmth of the mortal world.

通京桥
The Tongjing Bridge

　　通京桥始建于清代。木制的廊桥两端建有高耸的桥亭，覆盖着黛瓦的桥廊顶部如同一段隐藏于漫长山谷中的苍龙脊背。穿过桥亭走上桥，整个桥面如同一个坡形通道，缓慢而悠长。举目上望，满是木梁斗拱的桥屋，仿佛这是一个永远也走不到尽头的房间。桥内两侧成排的木凳，可坐于桥中凭栏而望，满眼尽是连绵山谷，安详而静谧。

　　几百年前建造此桥时，这里却是另一番喧闹繁华。周围不乏盐井、银矿，古商道繁忙，马队的铃声蹄音不断，因此那时这座桥也叫"通金桥"，它通的不只是金银财富，还通着边疆居民的情谊与希望。如今，运输与商贸早已有了别的承载工具，古桥也重归于寂然，守望着山谷溪流两岸的烟火人家，在质朴中寻找内敛的深度和沧桑的厚重。

The Tongjing Bridge was built in the Qing dynasty. Towering pavilions were built on both ends of the wooden veranda bridge. The roof of the veranda with black tiles is like the backbone of a dragon hidden in the long valley. Going through the pavilion and onto the bridge, the whole bridge looks like an aisle in the form of a slow and long slope. Looking up, you can see the bridge room built with beams and brackets, as if it was endless. There are rows of wooden benches on both sides of the bridge. You can sit on the bench and look against the balustrade at the serene valleys.

The area was noisy and bustling when the bridge was built centuries ago. Salt wells and silver mines dotted there. The ancient trade routes were busy and the bells and hooves of caravans rang continuously. Therefore, the bridge was also called the Tongjin Bridge (leading to gold). It not just led to wealth but also to the friendship and hopes of the frontier citizens. Now, transportation, commerce and trade have adopted and the ancient bridge resumed silence, looking at the mortal family on both banks of the stream in the valley and seeking the depth of restraint and the thickness of vicissitudes in simplicity.

05 藤桥
The Vine Bridges

云龙县水网纵横,又是群山巨壑的腹地,通向山外世界的道路很难走。但凭着对河那一边世界的渴望,对交流的期待,人们利用藤蔓架起一座座没有桥墩的藤桥,直至今日,这一根根盘曲藤蔓编织的桥仍然没有退出人们的生活。

藤桥这种原始而质朴的渡河工具,已有千年历史,由野藤经纬交织而成,且拴于桥两边根系发达的百年老树之上,有的桥上还铺有木板,每三五年更换一次野藤。这种不需一丝一毫人工材料的天然造桥方式,不由得让人赞叹古人与环境和谐共处的高妙智慧。沘江上至今仍有五座藤桥,它们保存完好且还在使用。藤桥上,常有服饰别致亮丽的本地各族乡民驮着背篓在荡悠悠间轻松谈笑而过。藤蔓密织的桥身如同一张牢固的网,将原生态的朴质美景网罗其中,只待人攀藤上桥去欣赏。

Yunlong County boasts dense water networks and is a hinterland of mountains and ravines. However, it is a harsh path to go from there to the outside world. Nonetheless, due to the thirst to know the world opposite the river and the expectations for exchanges, people set up vine bridges without piers. Even till now, these vine bridges still play a pivotal role in people's life.

Such vine bridges, as primitive and simple river-crossing tools boasting a history of up to 1,000 years, are made with wild vines and tied to century-old trees with deep roots on both sides of the bridges. Some bridges are paved with planks with wild vines replaced every three to five years. The natural bridge building method without any man-made materials arouses modern people's acclamation for the ingenuity and wisdom of the ancients for their harmonious co-existence with the environment. Five vine bridges still exist above the Bijiang River now, intact and in use. On the vine bridges, villagers of different ethnic groups wearing unconventional, pretty clothes often pass by talking smilingly and leisurely with pack baskets on their backs. The bridge bodies with dense vine netting show the originally ecological scenery for the appreciation of people on the vine bridges.

彩凤桥
The Caifeng Bridge

彩凤桥位于云龙县白石乡，此地自古因盐而富，进而文脉绵延、道德昌明。彩凤桥初建为石板桥，明代末年改建为有廊的风雨桥。人类营造桥梁是为了解决人类与自然的关系，也用来建立人与人之间的联系。

彩凤桥的桥身全部用木枋交错架叠，有顶的桥廊为行人遮光避雨，也有效保护了木制桥面免遭雨水风雷的侵袭。彩凤桥横跨四百余载依然坚固，远观之如同一只彩凤凌波而卧。古桥通行着两岸乡民，也方便犍牛骡马过桥。彩凤桥不但是古老村寨的公共空间，也是域内远接西藏，域外通至印度的必经桥梁。

桥亭之外直通村口，道路两旁古树参天，村内古寺香火鼎盛，古盐作坊等遗迹尚存，犹可见古沘江沿岸的经贸繁荣、文墨昌盛。

The Caifeng Bridge locates in Baishi Township, Yunlong County, which is rich for salt and features abundant culture and morality. Initially built as a stone bridge, it was rebuilt into a Fengyu bridge (a kind of covered bridge) in the late Ming dynasty. Bridges are built to handle the relations between human and nature and bridge connections between people.

The body of the Caifeng Bridge is composed of wooden cross frames, with the roofed veranda sheltering pedestrians from the sunlight and rain as well as the wooden bridge surface from the attack of rain, wind and thunder. The bridge with a history of more than 400 years is still firm now, looking like a colorful phoenix (caifeng) lying on the river in the distance. The ancient bridge links the villagers along both banks and facilitates the passage of bullocks and mules. The Caifeng Bridge is not simply the public space of the old village but also the inevitable linkage to Xizang within the country and India overseas.

The area outside the pavilion directly leads to the entrance to the village, with both sides of the road lined with towering trees. The ancient temple in the village thrives and the relics of ancient salt workshops still remain, showing the flourishing economy, trade and culture in ancient time along the banks of the Bijiang River.

西湖古桥群
The West Lake Ancient Bridge Cluster

映波桥、锁澜桥
The Yingbo Bridge and the Suolan Bridge

优美或壮丽的山水景色常常引来古人游憩，他们造桥修堤，吟诗作画。最终这些对自然的审美与互动融进了中国人的文化血脉。这也让名胜之地的桥梁脱离了桥本身的交通与建筑内涵，成为独立的历史文化风景线。

映波桥
The Yingbo Bridge

杭州西湖中的众多古桥就是这种人、文化、自然三者互动产生的动人建筑。著名诗人苏轼在杭州为官时，利用疏浚西湖时挖出的淤泥构筑出了一条贯穿西湖南北的大堤，世称"苏堤"。苏轼还给大堤上的六座桥赋予了诗意的名字——映波、锁澜、望山、压堤、东浦、跨虹。

映波、锁澜两桥，桥如其名。于映波桥上垂目观湖，无论是与桥毗邻的亭台楼榭，抑或是如雨丝飘荡的垂柳，诸般美景皆映于湖水中随波澜荡漾。锁澜桥则取锁住波澜之意。前者赏罢波影粼粼后，一过此桥，烟波荡漾的湖面便被锁在桥的一侧，其后的水面平静如镜，桥与桥影合璧于湖中。湖水如古镜，囊尽远山青翠、古塔梵铃，近处江渚坡岸，扁舟渔钓。

The splendid and gorgeous landscape often attracts the ancients to tour and rest. They built bridges and dykes, chanting and drawing pictures there. Finally, the aesthetics for nature and interaction with nature melted into the Chinese culture, making the bridge a scenery of history and culture besides its role in transportation and architecture.

The numerous ancient bridges over the West Lake of Hangzhou are touching architectures as results of the interactions between people, culture and nature. Prestigious poet Su Shi serving as an official of Hangzhou ordered to build a causeway, called Su Causeway by people in memory of him, linking the southern and northern West Lake using the dredge sludge of the West Lake. Su Shi gave poetic names to the six bridges on the causeway, namely, Yingbo Bridge, Suolan Bridge, Wangshan Bridge, Yadi Bridge, Dongpu Bridge and Kuahong Bridge.

The Yingbo Bridge and the Suolan Bridge are worthy of their names. Looking at the lake on the Yingbo Bridge, you can see neighboring pavilions, terraces and towers as well as weeping willows whose branches are drifting like rain. Such beautiful scenes are reflected in the lake and ripple with waves. The name of Suolan means locking the waves. The sparkling waves are "locked" at one side of the bridge and the other side of the lake surface is tranquil, with the bridge reflected in the lake. The lake is like an ancient mirror and reflects the images of mountains, trees, ancient pagodas and wind bells in the distance as well as islets, banks, and fishing men in skiffs in the vicinity.

02 望山桥、压堤桥、跨虹桥
The Wangshan Bridge, the Yadi Bridge and the Kuahong Bridge

　　古桥是中国古典审美中最具代表性的意象之一，出现在无数诗词歌赋、丹青妙笔之中。在这些艺术与诗性的表达中，桥可成为融于自然的风景，也可成为人类欣赏自然的一种工具。西湖苏堤诸桥便是如此。

　　望山桥可远眺西湖诸山，赏双峰插云，近观花港观鱼、三潭印月，四周山水江渚皆可入诗入画。压堤桥据传为眺望西湖全景的最佳之处，康熙皇帝也将"苏堤春晓"的景名立碑于此。跨虹桥位于苏堤最北端，是苏堤六桥中最长的一座。雨后长空彩虹飞架，凌空卧波当如此桥。古人爱用雨后出现的长虹来比作桥梁，这种将桥与自然融为一体的审美早已深深植根于中国人的审美之中，也印刻在那些千古流传的经典艺术作品中。

The ancient bridge as one of the most representative images in Chinese classical aesthetics often appears in a myriad of verses, ditties, odes and songs as well as drawings. In the artistic and poetic expressions, the bridge is a scene in nature and a tool for human to appreciate nature. The bridges of the Su Causeway of the West Lake is of this kind.

On the Wangshan Bridge, you can look at the mountains surrounding the West Lake and clouds over dual peaks in the distance and appreciate the sights of Viewing Fish at Flower Habor and Three Pools Mirroring the Moon in the vicinity. The mountains and rivers around can be written into poems or drawn into pictures. The Yadi Bridge is said to be the best place to have a panoramic view of the West Lake and the tablet of the scene Dawn on the Su Causeway in Spring autographed by Emperor Kangxi is erected there. The Kuahong bridge lies in the northernmost of the Su Causeway and is the longest among the six bridges of the Su Causeway, looking like a rainbow over the river after the rain. The ancients preferred to compare bridges to rainbow and the aesthetics of integrating bridge and nature has been long rooted in the mind of the Chinese and the classic artistic works handed down through the ages.

跨虹桥
the Kuahong Bridge

03 断桥
The Broken Bridge

　　西湖多桥,尤以断桥最为闻名。断桥并非桥断,而是指往孤山之路断于此桥。断桥得名于唐代。中唐诗人张祜在《题杭州孤山寺》中写道:"断桥荒藓涩,空院落花深。"到了宋代,断桥已经是方志与时人笔记中记录杭州时的代表性景观。多少文学作品都不乏对断桥风光的歌颂与描写,"断桥残雪"更是延续至今的建筑与自然之美合璧的典范景观。

　　断桥与爱情的结缘,始于元代的西湖竹枝词,这些诗歌中多以断桥比喻女子忠于爱情矢志不移的内心世界,也常描绘恋人在断桥幽会的甜蜜场景。而杭州西湖的白蛇传说,在千年之中逐渐演化为跨越世俗与种族的爱情主题。尤其是白蛇和许仙在断桥相遇的传说,使断桥成为中国文化中最为重要的爱情符号。透过西湖薄薄的雾霭与烟水,拨开千古神话低垂的帘幕,在断桥胜地寻找心灵的归宿、爱情的真意。

The West Lake boasts many bridges but the Broken Bridge is the most famous. The name Broken Bridge does not mean the bridge is broken. It means the path leading to Solitary Hill breaks here. The Broken Bridge got its name in the Tang dynasty. Poet Zhang Hu of the middle Tang dynasty period wrote in the poem "Inscription to the Solitary Hill Temple in Hangzhou": "The Broken Bridge is desolate with moss all around and flowers fell into the empty courtyard." In the Song dynasty, the Broken Bridge are a representative scene of Hangzhou, which is recorded in the local annals and notes. Eulogies and descriptions of the scenery of the Broken Bridge are written in many literary works. The Melting Snow at the Broken Bridge is a quintessential scene integrating the architectural and natural beauty even till now.

The ties between the Broken Bridge and love trace back to the West Lake folks of the Yuan dynasty. These songs often use the Broken Bridge as the symble of the absolutely determinded love of women. They also describe the sweet scenes of lovers meeting on the Broken Bridge quite a lot. The legend of the White Snake in the West Lake of Hangzhou gradually became the theme of love spanning different classes and ethnic groups. Especially, the legend of the White Snake and Xu Xian meeting on the Broken Bridge made the Broken Bridge the most important symbol of love in the Chinese culture. It is such a pleasure to raise the veil of the myth about the West Lake through the ages and seek the final destination of soul and true love at the scenic Broken Bridge.

04 长桥
The Long Bridge

　　长桥位于杭州西湖的东南角,是一座美丽的古典折桥。长桥虽为平梁折桥,长长的桥面也不乏平行于湖面的曲折线条,但人们生怕这平直的线条破坏了水景的灵秀,便在曲折之间加入了一处小小的桥拱和古亭。这番心思使得长桥在水面上高低起伏、曲折错落,也可以使游人的视角随移步而变化。

　　长桥古时又名双投桥,是为了纪念一对双双投湖的恋人——王宣教与陶师儿。著名的爱情悲剧《梁祝》中的"长桥相送"几乎是每个中国人耳熟能详的爱情典故。爱情的甜蜜使得再长的桥走起来也无比短,他们借长桥之"长"表达不愿与情人离别的苦痛心情。正值情浓之际,桥却已至尽头,方才了悟何谓长桥不长。细柳烟雨的阳春三月,或是飘雪狂风的凛凛寒冬,登桥伫立凝望,无尽遐想……

The Long Bridge in the southeast of the West Lake of Hangzhou is a beautiful classical zigzag bridge. Although it is a zigzag beam bridge and the long bridge surface features some curves parallel with the lake surface, people concerned that the straight lines might compromise the delicate beauty of the waterscape, so they built a small arch and a pavilion there to balance it out. The Long Bridge lies in undulation on the lake surface and the tourists can change their view while walking.

The Long Bridge was called Shuangtou Bridge in ancient times in honor of a couple named Wang Xuanjiao and Tao Shi'er drowning themselves for love. The episode "Send-off on the Long Bridge" in the famous love tragedy *The Butterfly Lovers* is an allusion of love familiar to almost every Chinese. Sweet love makes even the longest bridge seem short. The length of the Long Bridge was used to allude to the misery to part with the lover. With their most vehement love at heart, they suddenly found it was the end of the bridge and felt that the so-called Long Bridge was not long at all. You may fall into endless imagination when you stand in fixed gaze on the bridge either in warm spring with willows and rain or in bitterly chilly winter with drifting snow and fierce wind...

锦带桥
The Jindai Bridge

杭州西湖的白堤之上，有一座与断桥并称"姐妹桥"的锦带桥。因古时白堤一带名为十锦塘，此桥遂得名锦带桥。现存虽为清代桥梁式样，但明代时人的笔记杂谈中便有关于此桥的记载——此桥修造于北宋之前。清代康熙年间，始改为石拱桥，外形与断桥几近相同，所以，锦带桥与断桥有着"孪生姐妹"的说法，只是体量颇小。

锦带桥虽小，却极富意趣。盈尺小桥，一步可逾，前路曲径通幽，两边溪水潺潺，孤山似近在咫尺，平湖秋月风貌已在眼前，不但能点缀风景，亦为湖山盛景平添佳趣，更诠释着这里的风物与人情。时光荏苒，王朝兴废，古桥迭经修葺，已不复当年之态，但依然坚实和精致，静静安卧于白堤之上观春风冬雪，阅百态人生。

On the Bai Causeway of the West Lake in Hangzhou there's the Jindai Bridge which is a "sister bridge" of the Broken Bridge. Since the area around the Bai Causeway was called Shijin Pond in ancient times, the bridge got the name Jindai Bridge. Although it now displays the design of the Qing dynasty, the bridge was recorded in the notes of the Ming dynasty, which says that the bridge was built before the Northern Song dynasty. It was rebuilt into a stone arch bridge during the reign of Emperor Kangxi of the Qing dynasty resembling the appearance of the Broken Bridge. Therefore, the Jindai Bridge is considered as the "sister bridge" of the Broken Bridge despite its smaller architecture.

The Jindai Bridge was small in size, fairly interesting and easily accessible to the serene path ahead. With streams gurgling on both sides, the lonely mountain seems to be nearby and the moon is hanging over the peaceful lake of autumn. They not merely embellishing the scenery but also adding interest to the gorgeousness of the lakeside mountain and illustrating the scenery and human society there. The time zipped by and the dynasties rose and fell, the ancient bridge was repaired along the way and was not in its original form, but it is still solid and refined, lying quietly on the Bai Causeway to feel the spring wind, appreciate the winter snow and experience the colorful life of the human race.

通利桥
The Tongli Bridge

　　通利桥位于杭州西湖茅家埠，建于清中期以前。古时去天竺诸寺进香的香客们经常坐船到达通利桥后，从这里登岸，即便步行上香也会途经此桥。彼时的青石古桥台阶之上苔痕斑驳，桥拱高耸，乌篷扁舟穿梭其间，过客、乡民、游人的身影在桥上桥下来往不绝。每到此桥，即可静心屏气，把俗世中所有琐事和烦恼抛诸脑后，远处梵音袅袅从温润潮湿的空气中传来……

　　久远的场景虽逝，但古桥仍凝聚着人们对古老水乡的印象与畅想，带着典雅与宁静展示着水乡生活的前世今生。放下离尘出世的心，走过西湖杨柳依依的堤岸，跨过烟浪迷离的古桥，感受西湖的人文气息与文化意蕴。从此，对西湖那些精绝古桥多了一份眷念，对西湖美景也多了一丝牵挂。

The Tongli Bridge in Maojia Port of the West Lake in Hangzhou was built before the middle Qing dynasty. The pilgrims to the Tianzhu Temple and other temples in ancient times often came to the Tongli Bridge by boat and disembarked there. They would go past the bridge even when they went by land to the temples to pray. At that time, the mottled moss was on the green stone steps of the ancient bridge, the arches were tall, the black-awning boats shuttled in between and the passers-by, the villagers and the tourists came from and to the bridge in streams. Whenever on the bridge, you can hold your breath, cast the trifles and troubles to the wind and hear the Sanskrit drifting near from the moist air...

Although the remote scenes have vanished, the elegant and serene ancient bridge still bears people's impression and imagination of the ancient watertown and exhibits the present and past of the waterside life. Discarding the worldliness, you can go past the embankment lined with willows around the West Lake, cross the misty ancient bridge and experience the atmosphere of humanism and the cultural implications of the West Lake. From then on, you may think fondly of the exquisite ancient bridges and feel nostalgic about the amazing scenery of the West Lake.

泰顺廊桥
The Taishun Veranda Bridges

01

北涧桥
The Beijian Bridge

　　泰顺地处浙江南部，明代取"国泰民安、人心归顺"之意寓名。这里处群山峡谷之中，溪水蜿蜒逶迤，置身其间恍如隔世。山中乡民世代日出而作日落而息，耕作收获，生生不息。乡间生活中最跳跃的色彩、最有活力的舞台可能就是廊桥了。

　　北涧桥为叠梁式木拱廊桥，结构精巧，造型古朴。这座桥始建于康熙年间，后经六次重建，至今容颜不改，依然气势如虹。桥屋灰瓦红身，飞檐走兽，仰挽高天流云，俯视溪涧清波。桥旁古树掩映，青山绿水间，北涧桥显得异常绚丽，被誉为"世界上最美的廊桥"。

　　附近的村民自古以来在廊桥边耕作收割，洗衣担水，廊桥里面更是孩子们嬉戏的游乐场。尤其到了夏夜，远近村民于此聚会纳凉，一盘棋、一壶酒，几句戏文唱腔，多少坊间奇谈，都付与桥下潺潺流水。

Taishun in southern Zhejiang got its name in the Ming dynasty from the wish that "the country is prosperous and the people are at peace." You may feel as if being cut off from the outside world for ages when you stand in the mountains and valleys with the streams zigzagging in between. The villagers in the mountains set out to work at sunrise and return to rest at sunset, farming and harvesting continuously. The most dynamic stage with the most dynamic colors in rural life may be the veranda bridges.

    The Beijian Bridge is a wooden arch veranda bridge featuring an exquisite structure of post-and-linetel and an unsophisticated shape. The bridge was built during the reign of Emperor Kangxi and still keeps its appearance and magnificence after six times of maintenance. The red bridge house with gray tiles and overhanging eaves and beast statues looks up at the high sky and floating clouds and overlooks the mountain stream and clear waves. Ancient trees are hidden near the bridge and the Beijian Bridge looks extremely gorgeous in the green mountains and rivers and is reputed as the "most beautiful veranda bridge in the world."

    The villagers in the vicinity have been farming, harvesting, washing clothes and collecting water near the bridge since ancient times. The bridge is also the playground of the children to frolic. Especially, on a summer night, the villagers living far and near gather there to enjoy the coolness, play chess, drink a jug of wine, act in an play and tell fantastic stories, as heard by the gurgling stream under the bridge.

溪东桥
The Xidong Bridge

　　溪东桥始建于明，与北涧桥相去不远。两桥因造型颇为相似，故有"姐妹桥"之称。溪东桥桥心中段有三间高起的楼阁，两头翼角飞翘高挑，檐顶斗角绕云，青龙翘起，似在吞云吐雾。虹气临虚，影摇波月，桥旁建有道教的临水宫。

　　在古代中国，廊桥以其吸引人们驻留的优势成为与人们生活息息相关的公共建筑，这种公共性也使廊桥逐渐成为人们宗教信仰的投射地。人们希望桥梁在履行其交通和公共建筑作用的同时，还可为自己的日常生活带来一些福祉，于是在溪东桥的桥旁修建了一座庙宇，吸引了一方信众来此祭拜。古代此地村落的水口桥旁往往成为百姓的祭祀中心，承载着人们的信仰和世代的希望，也凝聚了廊桥千年不断的乡风民俗。

The Xidong Bridge built in the Ming dynasty is not far away from the Beijian Bridge. Similar in shape, the two bridges are called "sister bridges." Three high pavilions erect in the center of the Xidong Bridge, with upturned roof edges and eaves rolling around clouds and green dragons perking as if they are puffing the clouds. A riverside Taoist palace is built beside the bridge with its shadow waving on the water surface in the moonlight.

In ancient China, veranda bridges served as public architecture relating to people's life thanks to their ability of attracting people to stay. Such ability also made veranda bridges the center of people's religion and belief. People hoped that bridges could not simply facilitate transportation and function as public architecture but also benefit their religious life. A temple thus built beside the Xidong Bridge and attracted a large group of believers to pray there. The bridge in the village in ancient times was the center of sacrifice activities around, bearing the beliefs and hopes of different generations and boasting the folk customs nearby for thousands of years.

仙居桥、三条桥
The Xianju Bridge and the Santiao Bridge

中国古代先民以其卓绝的智慧才华,将房屋的建筑艺术和桥梁的结构造型有机融合,巧妙营造了中国特色的廊桥。仙居桥空灵高挑,行人走至桥中高耸的桥拱,不饰粉画的桥身木构件都能使人生出一种对古桥的崇敬之感。中国古诗词中颇具禅意的暮云、残阳、渔樵,在仙居桥畔皆可看到。这种飞桥无柱的编梁式木拱廊桥是廊桥的最高成就。曾经人们以为《清明上河图》中的虹桥,世间早已失传,却意外在荒草遍地的山涧溪流上觅得这千年飞虹。

三条桥虽与仙居桥颇似,但历史更为悠久,桥顶尚有大唐贞观旧瓦,不知其当年的盛唐形貌如今还有几分。随着现代文明步伐的疾速前行,古村萧索,驿道清冷,但凝聚着前人辛勤汗水和聪明智慧的古老廊桥,依然是本地乡民生活中的重要活动社交场所。桥上纳凉时传唱的家乡童谣,那一串串儿时的欢笑,那一串串魂牵梦萦的思念,蜕变成漂泊游子深深的乡愁,凝聚在古桥斑驳的桥梁、廊柱间。

仙居桥
The Xianju Bridge

With their excellent wisdom and talent, the Chinese ancients perfectly integrated the architectural art of houses and the bridge structure and exquisitely built the veranda bridges with Chinese characteristics. The Xianju Bridge erects high. When the pedestrians walk to the high arch in the center of the bridge, they can feel reverence for the ancient bridge because of the unadorned wooden structure. Such Buddhist images like the clouds at sunset, the setting sun, the fishing and the firewood in classical Chinese poetry can be seen at the side of the Xianju Bridge. This kind of architecture spanning over the river with waving wooden beams and no piers represents the highest architectural achievements of veranda bridges. People once thought that the rainbow-shaped bridge in the painting *Riverside Scene at Qingming Festival* had been long lost but then spotted this millennia-old "rainbow" over the mountain streams covered with weeds.

Looking similar to the Xianju Bridge, the Santiao Bridge has a longer history. There are still old tiles from the Zhenguan period of the Tang dynasty left on the top of the bridge. It makes people wonder whether its apperance in the flourishing Tang dynasty has kept till now. With the fast advancement of modern civilization, the ancient villages look desolate and the courier roads are silent. However, the ancient veranda bridges bearing the diligence and wisdom of the Chinese ancients are still important venues for the social life of the local villagers. The nursery rhymes singing on the bridge by villagers cooling the heat, the hearty laughter of the childhood and the missing in the dream turned into endless nostalgia of the wanderers and pervaded the mottled beam and veranda of the ancient bridge.

 刘宅桥、普宾桥、墩头桥、薛宅桥
The Liuzhai Bridge, the Pubin Bridge, the Duntou Bridge and the Xuezhai Bridge

刘宅桥
The Liuzhai Bridge

廊桥最明显的特征是桥上有长廊一般的屋顶，人可于桥中躲避风雨，纳凉休憩。因此廊桥两侧多有长长的条凳，可供行人歇息。逐渐地，廊桥从本乡居民的公共空间扩展成为四乡八镇的交通与贸易枢纽，桥内桥外成为了热闹的集市。大桥自不必说，即便如秀美小巧的刘宅桥，也在建筑形式上具备了可供交通、贸易、休憩的功能。

此类古桥还有普宾桥、墩头桥、薛宅桥等数座。古时，人们在旅途休息时可以在桥屋内买几块香喷喷的米糕吃，再去桥亭中的茶摊喝两碗茶，逛一逛桥边老街上的商铺，买几样时新的小玩意儿。乡民商贾、天涯旅人都在操劳与奔波之余暂落脚于此片刻，放下桥外世事多舛、忘记旅途风雨艰辛，从而使古桥成为心休憩的驿站。而今，桥上曾经熙攘热闹的商业区早已消失，不远处的荒草间偶然或可见到隐没其间的古驿道……

The most distinctive feature of veranda bridges is the veranda-like roof sheltering people from the wind, the rain and the sun. Therefore, many long benches were installed on both sides of veranda bridges for the rest of the pedestrians. Gradually, veranda bridges expanded from the public space of the villagers to the hub of transportation and trade of the towns and counties nearby. The area inside and outside the bridge became a busy market. Even the dainty Liuzhai Bridge can also be used for transportation, trade and rest as a roadside pavilion.

Such ancient bridges also include the Pubin Bridge, the Duntou Bridge and the Xuezhai Bridge. In ancient times, people could buy some rice cakes in the bridge house and have some tea in the bridge pavilion at the tea stand during their break while travelling. They could also buy some novel trinkets from the shops on the bridge-side streets. The villagers, merchants and travelers stayed there to relieve themselves of tiredness and forgot their adversities and hardships on the way. Now, the previously busy commerce on the bridge has long vanished, only leaving the ancient courier paths occasionally seen in the weeds.

永庆桥、霞光桥、南溪桥
The Yongqing Bridge, the Xiaguang Bridge and the Nanxi Bridge

廊桥不仅满足了人们跨越障碍的交通需要，本身也是能工巧匠理性思维与浪漫情怀的完美结合。许多廊桥高檐翘角、雕梁画栋，桥上亭阁间檐角交错，矗立于平静质朴的村落中异常醒目。

位于三魁镇的永庆桥华贵典雅，出檐深远，颇有大宋风雅之余韵。与此风格类似的还有精致秀丽的霞光桥，桥顶脊兽俏皮生动的南溪桥……它们或古朴大气，或雅致奇巧，但都巍峨挺拔。斑驳的梁栋彩画，掩映在桥头的两棵参天古树间；廊桥屋檐上形态夸张的脊兽和精致的雕花镂空悬鱼在古树的绿影摇曳中，若隐若现；桥下溪水涓涓，白鸭逐戏群鱼悠然而过。只要目之所及有古桥，便觉身处古意盎然的青绿宋画之中，一番人在画中游的意趣油然而生。青山秀水间一座座古桥将古人的审美、人与自然和谐共生的智慧悄然传承后世。

永庆桥
The Yongqing Bridge

Veranda bridges are not merely the structures for people to go across the rivers but also the perfect combination of rational thinking and the romantic feelings of the skillful craftsmen. Many veranda bridges have high and upturned eaves, carved beams and painted pillars. The bridge pavilions stood strikingly in the quiet, simple villages with the eaves of the bridge pavilions crossed.

The Yongqing Bridge in Sankui Town is luxuriousand elegant, with the eaves extending far and displaying the graceful style of the Song dynasty. The handsome Xiaguang Bridge and the Nanxi Bridge with good-looking and vivid statues of beasts engraved on the top of the verandas of the bridges boast a similar style. They are with either primitive simplicity and generosity or elegance and ingenuity, tall and upright. The mottled, colored paintings on the beams are hidden behind two towering ancient trees at the end of the bridge; the beasts carved in exaggerated shapes on the eaves of the veranda bridges and the exquisite hollowed-out hanging fish engraving indistinctly sway in the green shadow of the ancient trees; the stream gurgles under the bridge and white ducks leisurely pass the bridge chasing fish. While the ancient bridges are in sight, you will feel yourself in the dark green drawings of the style of the Song dynasty and a sense of fun travelling in the picture rises. The ancient bridges in the marvelous scenery quietly pass on the aesthetics of the ancients and their wisdom of seeking harmonious co-existence of human and nature to future generations.

第三章
Chapter 3

卧虹
The Lying Rainbow

古城名桥
Famous Bridges in Ancient Cities

清名桥
The Qingming Bridge

位于江苏无锡的清名桥始建于明万历年间,是一座花岗岩材质的单孔石拱桥,造型古朴匀称,稳固雄伟。无锡"寄畅园"的主人秦太清、秦太宁见塘河两岸交通不便,便捐资造桥,造福桑梓。两岸受益的民众从二人名字各取一字为桥命名"清宁桥"。及至清朝,因讳道光皇帝的名字"旻宁"而改名为清名桥。

清名桥是无锡古运河上一座规模最大、保存最完好、历史最悠久的单孔石拱桥,是中国古老运河历史的符号,也是江南繁荣的象征、水乡文化的缩影。立清名桥仰首远眺,京杭古运河缓缓流淌,西岸是熙攘南长街,东岸是灵秀南下塘,倚河而建的江南民居粉墙黛瓦,鳞次栉比,尽是"水弄堂"的独特景观。在悠然的夜色下,桥畔柳摇灯影乱,河心波漾月光悬,两岸的桨声、灯影、民居构成了一幅古运河"水上画廊"。

The Qingming Bridge in Wuxi of Jiangsu Province built in the Wanli period of the Ming dynasty is a single-arch bridge made of granite featuring simple and even modeling, firmness and magnificence. Qin Taiqing and Qin Taining, owners of Jichang Garden in Wuxi found the inconvenience of transportation between both sides of the artificial river and donated to build a bridge to benefit the fellow citizens. So the bridge was named Qingning Bridge after them by the people benefiting from the bridge. It was renamed into Qingming Bridge to avoid a taboo for the name of Emperor Daoguang in the Qing dynasty.

The Qingming Bridge, the largest and most intact single-arch stone bridge of the longest history on the ancient canal in Wuxi, is a symbol of the history of ancient Chinese canals and the prosperous Jiangnan Region, and the epitome of the riverside culture. Looking in the distance on the Qingming Bridge, the ancient Beijing-Hangzhou Canal slowly flows, with the bustling Nanchang Street on the western bank and the marvelous Nanxia Pond on the eastern bank. The rows upon rows of residential buildings built along the terrains of the river with white walls and black tiles formed the unique view of "water alley." On a leisurely night, willows sway and lamps flicker beside the bridge and waves glisten in the center of the river in the moonlight. The sound of paddles, the lamps and the residential buildings on both banks compose the "gallery of the waterside" on the ancient canal.

思本桥
The Siben Bridge

　　同里古镇街巷逶迤，河道纵横，自然有许多古桥，历史最久的当数思本桥。思本桥为南宋宝祐年间本地诗人叶茵所建，桥名取"当思以民为本"之意。思本桥是水乡常见的单孔拱形桥，桥身皆用武康石砌成。桥拱是标准的半圆拱，与水中倒影虚实相接，合成一环，波光粼粼中，更显秀丽优雅。

　　与古镇中繁华水岸一座座人来人往的桥相比，远在镇外的思本桥稍显落寞寂寥，少有游人会专门来此。古桥两旁遍披青藤枝蔓，微露半轨桥孔，桥上尽是岁月留下的斑驳痕迹和古色韵味，历经七百余年风雨，依然屹立在盈盈绿水之上，淡看浮华喧嚣。

The Tongli Ancient Town features winding streets, alleys, dense watercourses and thus many ancient bridges. Among them, the Siben Bridge is the one of the longest history. It was built by Ye Yin, a local poet in the Baoyou period of the Southern Song dynasty. The bridge name means "people-centered thinking." The Siben Bridge is a single-arch bridge commonly seen in the riverside region with the body built with Wukang stones. The arch is standard semicircular and forms a ring with its reflection in the water, looking extraordinarily beautiful in the glistening waves.

Compared with the bustling bridges in the ancient town, the Siben Bridge outside the town looks more lonely with little visit there. The semicircular bridge arch is slightly exposed among the green vines on both sides of the ancient bridge. With the mottled traces and lasting appeal, the bridge still stands on the limpid, green water and looks indifferently at the pomposity and din of the world after more than 700 years.

03 宝带桥
The Baodai Bridge

  位于苏州城东南的宝带桥，跨澹台湖，傍古运河，始建于唐代，距今已有一千二百多年了。相传，该桥当年为刺史王仲舒捐腰间镶玉宝带助资所建，故而得名"宝带桥"。此桥有五十三孔，为多孔联拱桥，全桥用坚硬素朴的金山石筑成，呈"宝带卧波"之长堤形，是现存的中国古代桥梁中最长的一座多孔石桥。

  宝带桥多孔联翩，倒映水中，虚实交映，有如苍龙浮水，又似鳌背连云，不仅为行人纤夫提供了方便，还为江南水乡增添了旖旎景色。每逢中秋，五十三个桥洞各衔一个明月，形成"宝带串月"的奇观。清乾隆皇帝经过此桥时也被这番景致打动，留下了"宝带春风波漾轻""涨痕犹见与桥平"的优美诗句。悠悠千载，宝带桥历经数度兴废，六次重修，依然横跨脉脉一水间，依稀是那白露染秋色，似那苍龙浮夕阳。

The Baodai Bridge in the southeast of Suzhou spanning over the Tantai Lake and besides the ancient canal was built in the Tang dynasty and has a history of more than 1,200 years. Legend has it that it was financed by the feudal provincial governor Wang Zhongshu who donated his girdle with embedded jade, hence its name Baodai (precious girdle) Bridge. The bridge has 53 arches as a multi-arch arch bridge. Built with hard, plain stones from the Jinshan Mountain, it looks like a prelious girdle on the waves. It is the longest existing multi-arch stone bridge among the ancient Chinese bridges.

The multi-arch Baodai Bridge is inverted into the river. With the virtual images in the water setting off, the bridge looks like a dragon floating on the river or a turtle with clouds on its back, not merely facilitating the passage of the pedestrians but also adding charm to the landscape of riverside towns in the Jiangnan Region. On Mid-Autumn Day, the bright moon can be seen through each of the 53 arches, forming the wonder of "A Bunch of Moons on the Precious Girdle." Emperor Kangxi of the Qing dynasty was amazed by the wonder when he went past the bridge, writing such wonderful verses as "The wind and the waves are light on the precious girdle" and "The trace of water rise is level to the bridge." The Baodai Bridge that has been repaired six times in its long history still spans over the lake in the autumn tainted by white dew like a dragon flying in the sunset.

04 迎仙桥
The Yingxian Bridge

迎仙桥位于浙江省新昌县，是中国国内首次发现的近似于悬链线拱的古石拱桥。而悬链线拱桥型是直到20世纪60年代才发明出来的先进桥梁科技。迎仙桥在明万历年间《新昌县志》中已有记载，现桥则是清道光年间重建的，比悬链线拱理论的传入足足早了一个世纪，填补了中国古桥技术史的空白。

时光悠然，古桥承载过无数脚印，抚摸过数度春秋，古代的能工巧匠虽然不一定掌握了悬链线拱的建筑理论，却已熟练掌握了它的建造技术。桥下惆怅溪依然碧水漾漾，桥上青石板满是斑驳痕迹，先人的智慧和精妙工艺并未随时间而漫漶。水桥相拥之间，古今相连，人桥交融。

The Yingxian Bridge in Xinchang County, Zhejiang is an ancient stone arch bridge whose arch is similar to the catenary arch, the first of its kind in China. The catenary arch bridge is a type of advanced bridge invented in the 1960s. The Yingxian Bridge was recorded in the *Annals of Xinchang County* in the Wanli period of the Ming dynasty. The present one was rebuilt in the reign of Emperor Daoguang of the Qing dynasty, one century earlier than the introduction of the theory of catenary arch and filled in the gap of the history of bridge building in ancient China.

Time elapses, ancient bridges have borne innumerable footsteps in so many years. Although the ancient skillful craftsmen did not necessarily master the catenary arch theory, they must had mastered its building technique. Blue stream water flows melancholy under the bridge and the green flagstones on the bridge are mottled. The wisdom and ingenious techniques of the ancients does not decrease or blur over the years. Water and bridges, the ancient times and the present, as well as human and bridges are soundly interconnected.

05 江东桥
The Jiangdong Bridge

　　江东桥亦名虎渡桥，始建于宋代，横跨在福建漳州东边的柳营江上，是世界最大最重构件的石梁桥。漳州，古时为闽南重镇，是福建乃至全国的重要交通枢纽。

　　史书有称"江南石桥，虎渡第一"。江东桥自肇建以来，屡有重修，古桥也由最早的浮桥变为木桥，最终演变成如今的石梁桥。这个过程历时七百余年，几经兴废，留下了不同朝代的石质构件，现有桥孔十九孔，每孔长短不一。江东桥的石梁每条重达两百吨，古代工匠们居然可以把它们架在波涛汹涌的急流之上，这至今令人惊叹。就连著名的英国学者李约瑟（Joseph Needham）也忍不住感叹道："江东桥是一个有趣的历史问题，在中国的其他地方和国外的任何地方都找不到可同它相比的。"

The Jiangdong Bridge, also called Hudu Bridge and built in the Song dynasty, spans over the Liuying River east of Zhangzhou, Fujian as the worldwide largest and heaviest stone beam bridge. Zhangzhou, a pivotal town in southern Fujian in ancient times, is now an important hub of transportation in Fujian and even in the whole country.

It is recorded in history that "The Hudu Bridge is the No.1 stone bridge in the Jiangnan Region." Since its initial construction, the Jiangdong Bridge has been repeatedly rebuilt and the ancient bridge changed from a floating bridge at the earliest to a wooden bridge later then a stone beam bridge now, covering a period of more than 700 years and leaving stone structures of different dynasties and 19 arches of diverse lengths. Each beam of the Jiangdong Bridge weighs up to 200 tons but the ancient craftsmen could astonishingly put them up over the torrential currents. Even prestigious British scholar Joseph Needham could not help saying: "The Jiangdong Bridge is an interesting historical question and cannot be compared in any other places in China and beyond."

太仓石拱桥
The Taicang Stone Arch Bridges

　　太仓是长江三角洲的水乡，形态纷呈、独具特色的明清临水建筑，悠长的老街，古朴雄浑的古桥，处处散发出江南小镇淳朴的魅力。古桥是太仓的一大特色，它们是古镇活的历史。在太仓众多的桥梁中，最有名的便是周泾桥、皋桥、州桥这三座始建于元代的古桥。

　　周泾桥以青石建造，桥上还有元代栏板石，两侧雕饰着精美的牡丹、缠枝莲和游嬉的瑞兽，灵动传神，线条流畅，更显古桥端庄大气。皋桥是一座单孔石拱桥，桥身全部以青石砌筑。州桥原名安福桥，因桥心正对州府门，故更名州桥，桥原本有三孔，现仅存中孔。这三座古桥迈过八百载春秋的浩荡，载着花瓣的涟漪，在淅淅沥沥的细雨声中，成为江南水乡的经典图景。

Taicang is a riverside city in the Yangtze River Delta. The riverside architecture of different shapes and unique characteristics, the long, old streets and the simple, mighty ancient bridges give out the unadorned charm of the small riverside town of the Jiangnan Region. Ancient bridges are one of the major characteristics of Taicang and are a part of the history of the ancient town. Among the numerous bridges in Taicang, the most famous ones are the Zhoujing Bridge, the Gaoqiao Bridge and the Zhouqiao Bridge which were all built in the Yuan dynasty.

The Zhoujing Bridge was built with bluestones and has some balustrades of the Yuan dynasty on the bridge. Peonies, lotuses and frolicking as well as vivid auspicious beasts exquisitely engraved with smooth lines on both sides highlight its dignity and grandeur. The Gaoqiao Bridge is a single-arch stone bridge built with bluestones. The Zhouqiao Bridge originally named Anfu Bridge was renamed because the center of the bridge was just opposite of the gate to the Zhou (state) goverment. The bridge originally had three arches but only the middle arch remains now. The three ancient bridges undergoing the vicissitudes of more than 800 years compose classic misty riverside scenery of the Jiangnan Region.

07 都江堰南桥
The South Bridge of Dujiangyan

　　都江堰南桥俗称"南桥",始建于清代光绪年间。南桥是一座恢宏壮丽的廊桥,桥上建筑有着浓厚的巴蜀建筑风格,高翘的檐角如一只只展翅欲飞的大雁。桥身、桥廊上装饰着木雕、彩绘等琳琅满目的艺术品,细节考究,优美典雅。清澈的岷江水从桥下湍急而过,都江堰南桥如同一座"水上画楼"。

　　南桥虽经战乱及汶川地震重创,但仍屹立不倒。如今,修复后的南桥凌空而越,尤其入夜之后,桥上灯火璀璨,桥下江中倒影粼粼。南桥夜色遂成为当地不可不游的夜景,梦幻的灯光随着桥下滚滚江水流向远方,也流入人们心中。

The South Bridge of Dujiangyan, which is commonly known as the South Bridge, was initially built in the reign of Emperor Guangxu of the Qing dynasty. It is an imposing veranda bridge of the strong architectural style of Ba Shu (two ancient states in Sichuan). The upturned eaves look like wild geese. The bridge body and veranda are embellished with dazzling artworks such as wood carvings and colored paintings with particular details and gracefulness. The limpid water of the Minjiang River roars in torrents and the South Bridge is like a gallery on the water.

The South Bridge went through wars and the Wenchuan Earthquake but still erects today. Now, the repaired South Bridge soars aloft. Especially, the reflections glisten in the river under the bridge when the lights are turned on in the evening. The night scene of the South Bridge is a must see and the fantastic light flows afar with the rolling river and into the bottom of people's heart.

08 青岛栈桥
The Qingdao Zhanqiao Bridge

  青岛栈桥始建于光绪年间，原是军事专用人工码头建筑，后来逐渐成为一座观景名桥。桥身从海岸探入如弯月般的青岛湾深处。桥南端筑半圆形防波堤，堤内建有中式风格的两层八角楼——"回澜阁"。登楼远眺海景，但见海天一色，层层巨浪卷来，海洋宽广博大的气息瞬间萦绕全身，"飞阁回澜"由此成为"青岛十景"之一。

  19世纪末，栈桥那美丽浪漫的身影逐渐变成了人们印象中青岛的视觉标志。栈桥既是这座城市的主权象征，也是近代中国城市化的一段注脚。上百年来，人们在这座长长的桥上观旭日、听晚潮，桥上的人流风景，日日不同；桥上的过客背影，个个迥异。栈桥浸泡在潮起潮落和斑斑驳驳的陈年往事中，悄悄留给桥上人一个可以抛却烦愁与忧伤的心灵角落。

    The Qingdao Zhanqiao Bridge initially built in the reign of Emperor Guangxu was originally a man-made military wharf and gradually became a famous sight. The bridge body penetrates into the distance of the moon-shaped Qingdao Bay from the seacoast. The south part of the bridge is a semicircular breakwater including the Huilan Pavilion, a two-story octagon house in the Chinese style. Looking at the seascape from the pavilion, you can see the sea and the sky merged into one. Waves come and the vast and extensive sea surrounds you. The Qingdao Zhanqiao Bridge is hence one of the Ten Famous Scenes of Qingdao.

    In the late 19th century, the beautiful and romantic Zhanqiao Bridge gradually became the visual sign of Qingdao in people's impression. The Zhanqiao Bridge symbolizes the sovereignty of the city and a landmark of the urbanization of modern China. For centuries, people come to this long bridge to watch the sunrise and listen to the evening tide, composing a different view on the bridge every day with different backpackers coming and going. Witnessing the ebb and flow and the past events, the Zhanqiao Bridge offers an outlet for the people on the bridge to ditch their worries and sorrows.

09 双龙桥
The Double Dragon Bridge

　　双龙桥位于建水古城城西的泸江与塌冲河上,因两河蜿蜒如游龙故而得名。建水古城是古代蜀地去往越南的要津,而双龙桥是入建水城的必经之地。该桥于清乾隆年间先建三孔,道光年间续建十四个桥孔与原有的三孔首尾相连,合为一体,故又称"十七孔桥"。桥的一端建有圆形的尖顶桥亭。桥面中心三座歇山重檐的阁楼连缀在一起,楼楼相映。玲珑精致的楼阁和雄伟壮丽的长桥相连,安闲地静卧在蓝天之下碧波之上。漫步桥上,走进桥楼,在雕刻精致的隔扇花窗之间可观旁楼,亦可阅江水。无论是楼中观楼,抑或是楼中观水,都恰似踏虹行空。泸江、塌冲河二水从远方滚滚而来,在脚下汇合又一泻千里,氤氲出古今皆通的清新雅韵。

The Double Dragon Bridge built over the Lujiang River and the Tachong River in the west of the Ancient City of Jianshui got the name because the two rivers wind like dragons. The Ancient City of Jianshui was a key post from Sichuan to Vietnam in ancient times and the Double Dragon Bridge was inevitable entering Jianshui. Only three arches were built in the reign of Emperor Qianlong of the Qing dynasty and fourteen arches were added to the former three in the reign of Emperor Daoguang, hence it got another name Seventeen-arch Bridge. A pavilion with a round pinnacle was built at one end of the bridge. Three pavilions with double gable-and-hip roofs are connected in the center of the bridge side by side. The exquisite pavilion and the magnificent long bridge are linked and leisurely lie below the blue sky and above the green waves. Slowly walking on the bridge and into the bridge pavilion, you can see other pavilions or the rivers through the ingeniously engraved partition boards and lattice windows as if you were walking on the rainbow. The water from the Lujiang River and the Tachong River rolls in, converges underfoot, flows down vigorously and gives off the freshness and elegance in ancient and modern society.

龙脑桥
The Longnao Bridge

在四川泸县北郊九曲河上，有一座修建于明代洪武年间的龙脑桥。这座石墩石梁式平桥，风格浑厚刚毅。十四座桥墩之中的八座桥墩依次雕有龙、狮、象、麒麟等瑞兽，巨大的瑞兽群雕是这座古桥最精彩之处，在中国古桥中也极为罕见。这些承托着石桥与桥上行人的瑞兽造型精美、情态传神，令人惊叹几百年前先人雕刻技艺之精湛。它们的眼耳鼻眉样貌逼真，口中所含之珠仍可滚动，周身的鳞翅线条流畅，造型写实之余却又不失想象与夸张的艺术韵味。几百年寒来暑往，古桥苔痕越发青翠，遥望远山环伺，树木参天，桥下河水清澈，鉴照出石桥的倒影。

On the Jiuqu River of the northern suburbs of Luxian County, Sichuan, there is the Longnao Bridge built in the Hongwu period of the Ming dynasty. The stone pier and beam flat bridge displays vigor and resoluteness. The eight out of 14 piers of the bridge are in the shapes of such auspicious beasts as dragons, lions, elephants and Qilin. The huge sculptures of auspicious beasts are the most wonderful attractions of the ancient bridge and are rarely seen in ancient Chinese bridges. The auspicious beasts bearing the pedestrians on the stone bridge and the bridge itself are of fine shapes and vivid postures, indicating the amazing engraving technique of the predecessors centuries ago. The beasts' eyes, ears, noses and eyebrows are true to life, the stone pearls in their mouths can roll, the lines of scaly wings are smooth and their modeling is life-like, at the meantime full of imagination and exaggerated artistic style. With the passing of time over centuries, the moss on the ancient bridge has turned increasingly verdant. Seen in the distance, the bridge is surrounded by mountains and towering trees, with the reflection of the stone bridge in the limpid water under the bridge.

清华彩虹桥
The Qinghua Rainbow Bridge

　　在江西婺源，随处都可以邂逅古道亭桥，其中有一座极其古老的廊桥——清华彩虹桥。这座廊桥的名字出自唐诗"两水夹明镜，双桥落彩虹"。古桥始建于南宋，条石垒成的四个巨大船型桥墩，宛如碉堡，厚重敦笃，可缓冲洪水肆虐时的冲击。桥墩上建亭，桥墩与桥墩间以廊相连，形成六亭五廊的格局，宛若彩虹落人间，美丽绝伦。人踏彩虹桥而上，看亘古沧桑之水，听桥边水车声悠扬，眺望远山苍翠，赏婺源的油菜花海，留在人心中的便不仅仅是古老的厚重，更有一份悠远的浪漫。

　　Ancient paths, pavilions and bridges can be seen everywhere in Maoyuan, Jiangxi, including the Qinghua Rainbow Bridge, an ancient veranda bridge. The bridge got the name from the Tang verse "The lake between the two rivers looks like a mirror, and the two bridges on the river are like two fallen rainbows." The ancient bridge was built in the Southern Song dynasty. The four giant boat-shaped piers built with stone strips look like stately forts and can buffer the impact of rampant floods. Pavilions were built on the piers which are connected with verandas, forming the pattern of six pavilions connected with five verandas and looking like rainbows in the paradise with matchless beauty. Stepping on the Rainbow Bridge, you can see the immemorial water, hear the melodious sound of the waterwheel near the bridge, look at the distant mountains and verdant trees and appreciate the sea of rape flowers in Maoyuan, leaving not merely the dignity of the past but also the romance of the time in your heart.

安澜索桥
The Anlan Cable Bridge

　　安澜索桥也称"安澜桥",始建年代不详,但早在唐代时,它就已经在都江堰之上和着唐诗的韵律诗意地摇荡了。安澜索桥飞架岷江南北,是中国索桥的典范之作,也是古代四川西部与阿坝之间的交通要道。安澜索桥曾是以木为桩、以竹为缆,"编竹绳跨江"的竹索桥,历经多番改建,索桥形态一直未变。

　　如今的安澜桥铁索凌空,横置渠首,登索桥,上可观分水鱼嘴,下可览宝瓶口,堤、堰、口,都江堰水利工程的奇迹全貌尽收眼底。千百年来,索桥静默,与下方浩荡奔流的岷江水相互守望,用微晃的身躯支撑着行人匆匆的脚步和每天的日升月落。

The time when the Anlan Cable Bridge, also called Anlan Bridge, was built is unknown. But it had already existed on Dujiangyan amid the poetic rhymes of the Tang poetry as early as the Tang dynasty. The Anlan Cable Bridge over the Minjiang River is the quintessence of the Chinese cable bridge and was also a vital communication line between the western Sichuan and Aba area in ancient China. The Anlan Cable Bridge is a bamboo cable bridge over the river with wooden balusters and bamboo cables. Rebuilt repeatedly, it still maintains its original cable bridge form. Now, the cables of the Anlan Bridge is high up in the air and over the river. Climbing onto the cable bridge, you can see the Fish-Mouth-Shaped Water Diversion Weir and the Bottleneck Channel of Dujiangyan. You can have a panoramic view of the wonders of Dujiangyan composed of dams, weirs and cannels. For thousands of years, the cable bridge is quiet, keeping watching the rushing Minjiang River under it and bearing the hurried footsteps of the pedestrians and the everyday sunrise and sunset.

13 方顺桥
The Fangshun Bridge

　　方顺桥位于河北省保定市，始建于西晋永嘉三年（309），是中国有文字记载的最早的桥。古时候，方顺桥是南北驿路交通必经之地，历代都是重要关隘。方顺桥为三孔石桥，现存桥体为明代重修。桥拱由长方形料石悬砌，桥面由长条石铺垫，桥两端各有两个造型古朴的巨狮，分踞左右。方顺桥浑厚端庄，造型优美且坚固耐用。桥上栏杆柱头的石狮子虽经风霜却依旧灵动，静观京畿重地千年风云变幻。如今，伴随着桥下水道的干涸，历经繁华的方顺桥更多了几分孤寂、沉静与冷清，与南岸不远处国道上的车流往来形成了鲜明对比。虽然方顺桥变天堑为通途的咽喉功能已不复存在，但那厚重沧桑的风采却历久弥新。

The Fangshun Bridge in Baoding, Hebei initially built in the Yongjia period of the West Jin dynasty (309) is the earliest bridge in China as recorded. In ancient times, the Fangshun Bridge was inevitable on the south-north post road and a pivotal pass in all dynasties. The Fangshun Bridge is a three-arch stone bridge and the present bridge body was rebuilt in the Ming dynasty. The arches are made of rectangular dressed stones. The bridge surface is paved with long stone strips. Two giant stone lions of simple modeling crouch on both sides of the bridge respectively. The solemn, sturdy and durable Fangshun Bridge features a handsome model. The weathered stone lions on the pillars of the bridge still look lively and silently observe the changes of Baoding for thousands of years. Now, as the watercourse under the bridge dries up, the previously bustling Fangshun Bridge is desolate, quiet and lonely, forming a stark contrast with the traffic flow on the national road not far away on the south bank. Although the Fangshun Bridge is no longer a strategic position, its profound mien is everlasting.

14 银锭桥
The Yinding Bridge

　　北京什刹海有一座建于明代的单孔石拱桥，南北横跨在前海与后海交汇处的水道上，桥身以青石为材，因整座桥酷似倒置的银元宝，故取名银锭桥。由于其地风光旖旎，最是京城内风雅去处，有明以来，对它的称颂不绝于史，《燕都游览志》称其为"城中水际看山第一绝胜处也"。于是上自达官显贵，下至平民百姓，闲暇之余都爱来此游玩赏景。久而久之，此处热闹繁华名闻京城，更因靠近皇家宫苑，而成为领略帝京繁华的好去处。

　　今日的银锭桥下水波粼粼，桥畔杨柳夹岸，葱茏流翠；桥周围古宅相拥，胡同密集，古韵悠然；隐于浓荫中的王府、寺庙的屋顶飞檐依稀可见，一派清雅幽静的氛围。入夜，此地则更是游人夜赏游玩的绝佳之处。几百年中以此为主题的艺术作品更是不知凡几，绘画、电影、戏剧……银锭桥总是能给艺术家无尽的灵感。

　　There is a single-arch stone bridge built in the Ming dynasty in Shichahai of Beijing, spanning over the watercourse at the intersection of Qianhai Lake and Houhai Lake in the south-north direction. The bridge made of bluestones looks like a shoe-shaped silver ingot and hence got the name "Yinding (silver ingot) Bridge." Thanks to its surrounding's lovely scenes, it is the most elegant sight in Beijing. Praises for it have been pouring since the Ming dynasty. The *Records of Tourism in Beijing* describes it as "the best place to see mountains by the river in the city." For this reason, people of all walks of life love to tour there in their spare time. As time passed, the liveliness and prosperity there are widely known in the capital city. It becomes the best place to view the bustling capital because of its vicinity to the imperial palace.

　　Now, the water under the Yinding Bridge glistens and willows line both banks of the bridge, presenting a verdant sight; the ancient houses around the bridge embrace each other and the alleys densely cluster with archaic charm; the palaces of princes hidden in dense shades and the overhanging eaves of the temples can be faintly seen, presenting a refined, serene atmosphere. It is the best place to tour and appreciate the night scenes. Numerous artworks on this theme have been worked out during centuries, such as paintings, movies, dramas... The Yinding Bridge can always arouse the inspirations of the artists.

15 波日桥
The Bori Bridge

波日桥位于四川甘孜州，横跨雅砻江，是我国目前年代最久、保存最完整、跨度最大的伸臂式木石质结构桥，被誉为"康巴第一桥"。据史料记载，波日桥始建于元末明初，相传是藏族建筑大师唐东杰布设计的。波日桥由桥身、桥墩、桥亭三部分构成，全部由木头、石块和树藤相间叠砌而成，没用一钉一铆，堪称鬼斧神工。波日桥的桥面高悬在湍急江水之上，充满了飞扬的美感，故有"飞桥"之美誉。古桥粗犷厚重，整齐美观，几百年来造福了雅砻江两岸的乡民。

The Bori Bridge in Ganzi Prefecture of Sichuan spanning over the Yalong River is the semi-girder, wooden and stone bridge of the longest history, the most intact preservation and the largest span in China, hence it is famed as the "No.1 Bridge of Kham." According to the historical records, the Bori Bridge was initially built in the late Yuan and early Ming dynasties and was said to be designed by Xizang architect Don Dongjeb. The Bori Bridge is composed of body, piers and pavilions and is built with wood, stones and vines, without a nail and a rivet with such uncanny workmanship. The surface of the Bori Bridge is suspended high over the rushing river, generating a strong sense of beauty, hence its reputation "the Flying Bridge." The ancient bridge looks rough, dignified, neat and beautiful, benefiting the villagers on both banks of the Yalong River over centuries.

琉璃河石桥
The Stone Bridge over the Liuli River

　　琉璃河石桥又称"燕谷长桥",横跨北京南部的琉璃河上。石桥始建于明朝嘉靖年间,是一座有十一个桥孔的南北向联拱桥,桥身全部用巨大的石块砌筑,悠长的桥面平坦舒缓。桥上的实心栏板和栏杆上雕刻着海棠纹饰,望柱柱头雕饰覆莲花。桥下潺潺河水挽着浪花,叙述着古老的历史,夜晚的明月照遍古桥几百年来的桥面清霜。曾经的万柳萦堤如今依旧,历经风雨沧桑的石桥也依然稳固如初。琉璃河石桥满载画意诗情,抚今追昔,可观历史之沧桑;继往开来,可察时代之变迁。

The Stone Bridge over the Liuli River, also called Yangu Long Bridge, spans over the Liuli River in southern Beijing. Initially built in the Jiajing period of the Ming dynasty, it is an eleven-arch arch bridge lying south to north, made of giant stones and featuring an even, long surface with a slight slope. The solid balustrades and the balusters on the bridge are engraved in the pattern of Chinese cherry-apples with the pillars in the design of lotus flowers. The gurgling water and the waves under the bridge narrate ancient history and the bright moon at night shines on the bridge surface for centuries. The past embankment surrounded by willows remains the same today and the weather-beaten stone bridge is still as firm as before. The scene of The Stone Bridge over the Liuli River is still poetic and can reflect the vicissitudes in history; well-kept ahead, it will bear witness to the changes of the times.

永通桥
The Yongtong Bridge

　　永通桥始建于唐永泰年间，桥名取"永远通济"之意。永通桥历代屡有重修，但桥身主体始终保持了宋以前的风格，雕饰多具明代风貌。永通桥的艺术风格和桥梁结构形式与赵州桥近似，虽不若赵州桥大气磅礴，却自有一番优美秀雅、空盈灵秀。桥上石雕的装饰图案种类繁多，团花、飞马、游鱼、河神、瑞兽、狮子等，皆细腻精致、线条流畅。透过薄薄的雾霭与烟水，拨开桥畔垂柳柔细的帘幕，古桥跨在蜿蜒的冶河之上，栖息于时光深处，淡然看尽俗世繁华。

The Yongtong Bridge built in the Yongtai period of the Tang dynasty got a name meaning "permanent connection." Although rebuilt several times, the main body of the bridge still keeps the style before the Song dynasty while the engraved embellishments mostly reflect the style and features of the Ming dynasty. The artistic style and the structure of the Yongtong Bridge are similar to those of the famous Zhaozhou Bridge. Not as mighty and imposing as the Zhaozhou Bridge, it is beautiful, elegant and gorgeous. There are various designs on the stone engravings of the bridge, including flower clusters, dashing horses, swimming fish, river god, auspicious beasts and lions, all exquisitely engraved with smooth lines. Through thin mist and foggy water as well as the curtain of riverside willows, the ancient bridge spans over the zigzag Yehe River, perches in the depth of time and looks indifferently at the bustling world.

卞桥
The Bianqiao Bridge

　　卞桥据考始建于晚唐时期，坐落于山东泗水县，是山东现存最古老的桥梁。这座三孔石拱桥横跨于泗河上游，造型端庄，风格华丽。每块栏板上雕刻着精美浮雕，雕凿技法精湛。抚摸着带有岁月厚重痕迹的栏杆莲花柱头，行走在古老的卞桥上，就像穿行在千年的时光里。桥拱顶端的神兽从桥身中探出头去，凝视着滔滔不绝的流水，无论是水面的清波荡漾，还是两岸垂柳依依，似乎都被它圆睁的眸子看尽。

　　每逢中秋之夜，明月高照，桥下水中便会映出两轮明月，如诗如画，此景被称作"卞桥双月"，故而卞桥又有"双月桥"之称。扶雕栏，临玉水，披一身银色月光，这种浪漫引来古今多少文人墨客在桥上把酒望月，低吟浅唱。那份热闹、熙攘和诗意如今又安在哉？唯有当年桥上月，夜深还到水西头。

The Bianqiao Bridge initially built in the late Tang dynasty and sitting in Sishui County of Shandong Province is the oldest bridge existing in Shandong. The three-arch stone bridge spans over the upper reaches of the Sihe River, featuring a solemn model and a resplendent style. Each balustrade is engraved with fine reliefs chiseled with superb craftsmanship. Touching the lotus-shaped heads of the balusters with the marks of years and walking on the ancient Bianqiao Bridge, you seem to travel in time of thousands of years. The mythical creatures on top of the bridge arch pop their heads out from the body of the bridge and gaze at the gushing water, the rippling waves and the willows on both banks with their round eyes.

The moon is bright on the night of Mid-Autumn Day. Two images of the moon will be reflected poetically on the water surface under the bridge. The scene is called Twin Moons at the Bianqiao Bridge, thus the Bianqiao Bridge is also called the Twin Moons Bridge. Feeling the balustrades at the riverside and wearing the silvery moonlight all over, men of letters since ancient times have been attracted by the romance there to drink wine and chant in a low voice while appreciating the moon. Where are the past liveliness, bustle and poetic flavor now? Only the moon above the bridge still shines to the western part of the river at night.

19 永镇桥
The Yongzhen Bridge

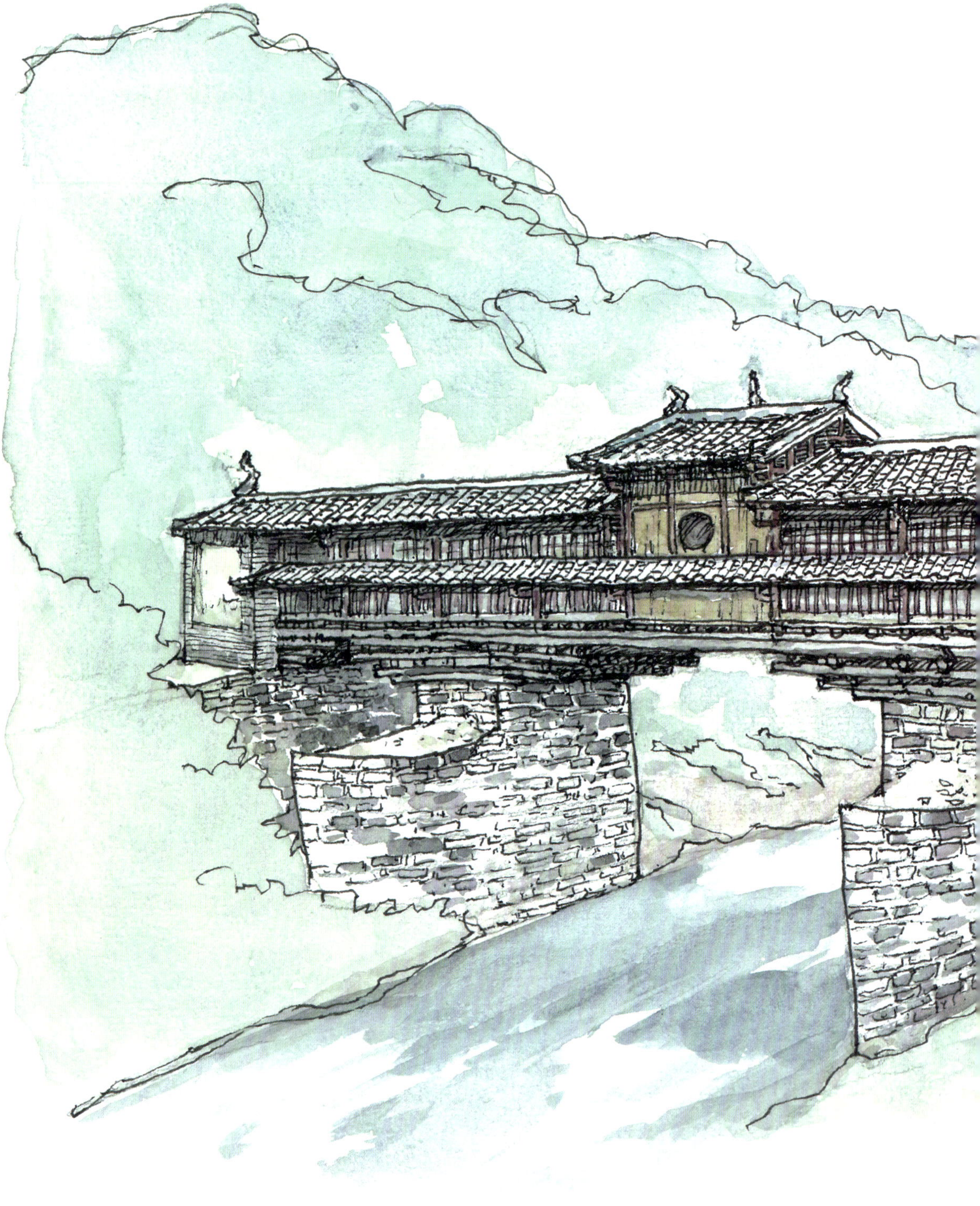

永镇桥位于江西省赣州市安远县，始建于清顺治年间，由高僧募资建造，是江西省现存罕见的石墩木梁悬臂式廊桥。这座古朴端庄的廊桥具有浓厚客家建筑风格，层见叠出的杉木悬臂梁承托着桥面，其上建木廊黛瓦的桥廊，因此桥面犹如一间长长的房屋，别具一格。朴素无华的石砌船型桥墩默默立于潺潺河水之中，静候着雨季的激浪拍打。

　　永镇桥倚山跨水，两岸是密密的芦苇，掩映了世事的匆匆，周围环绕的青山驻守着萧瑟的古驿道。永镇古桥历沧桑而不败，瞻风华而仍存。站在桥上，唯觉山水之苍茫，天地之高远；慨叹时光之迅疾，岁月之悠远。如今，古道湮灭，古村落搬迁，饱受风霜的永镇桥不再是熙攘古道上的交通要冲，但它深隐在群峰林泉中，仙灵秀逸，遗世独立。

　　The Yongzhen Bridge in Anyuan County, Ganzhou, Jiangxi, initially built in the reign of Emperor Shunzhi of the Qing dynasty with the fund raised by an eminent monk, is a rarely seen cantilever veranda bridge with stone piers and wooden beams existing in Jiangxi. The primitive, dignified veranda bridge was built in a strong architectural style of the Hakkas, with overlapping fir cantilever beams supporting the bridge surface. With a wooden veranda and black tiles, the bridge surface seems to be a long, distinctive house. The plain, unadorned boat-shaped stone piers quietly stand in the gurgling river and wait for the hit of surfs in rainy seasons.

　　The Yongzhen Bridge leaning against mountains and spanning over the river with dense reeds on both banks set off the fast steps of human life. The surrounding green mountains safeguard the bleak ancient post roads. The ancient Yongzhen Bridge still erects despite the vicissitudes and its elegance still lingers on. Standing on the bridge, you can only feel the vast landscape and the far-away heaven and earth; you will lament with sighs for the fast elapse of time and the remote years. Now, the ancient paths have vanished, the ancient villages have been relocated and the weathered Yongzhen Bridge is no longer a communication hub on the bustling ancient path. However, hidden in the mountains, it is still delicately beautiful and remains aloof from the world.

20 地坪风雨桥
The Diping Fengyu Bridge

　　"风雨桥"作为侗族最具特色的代表性建筑之一,因桥上建有长廊和桥楼,青瓦覆盖,可挡风遮雨,故而得名。风雨桥既是当地民众出行的交通设施,也是附近几个村寨重要的公共空间。地坪风雨桥位于贵州省黎平县地坪镇,始建于清光绪年间,桥上建有三座飞檐重重的桥楼,桥廊屋脊上泥塑鳌鱼、抢宝的双龙、翱翔的双凤形象鲜活灵动,雕刻精湛华丽。桥廊的木构件上绘有各类历史人物故事彩画和卷草花纹等。风雨桥年代久远,桥身苔痕斑驳,给人一种劫后余生的古朴苍凉之感。在贵州黎平的侗寨,浸透古韵的风雨桥与巍然屹立的鼓楼交相辉映,在历史的沧桑巨变中,侗族人将古老的文化风情用这样唯美的方式一代代传承,时间在这里,仿佛不曾流逝。

One of the representative architecture with the characteristics of the Dong nationality, the Fengyu Bridges got the name because of their verandas and bridge towers covered with gray tiles can shelter people from the wind (feng) and the rain (yu). The Fengyu Bridge is both a structure for the locals to travel and an important public space of the villages nearby. The Diping Fengyu Bridge in Diping Town, Liping County, Guizhou was built in the reign of Emperor Guangxu of the Qing dynasty. Three bridge towers with overlapping eaves are built on the bridge and clay figurines of fish, two dragons scrambling for a pearl and two soaring phoenixes are vividly and delicately engraved on the ridge of the veranda. Colored paintings about various historical figures and stories as well as curly grass patterns are painted on the wooden structures of the veranda. The mottled, desolate Fengyu Bridge generates a sense of simplicity and bleakness after a disaster. In the Dong village, Liping County, Guizhou, the antique Fengyu Bridge and the tower standing majestically add radiance to each other. In the radical changes of history, the Dong people have passed on the ancient culture in this artistic manner. It seems that time does not elapse there.

21 葛镜桥
The Gejing Bridge

贵州福泉城东南麻哈江两岸绝壁之上，有一座载入中国桥梁史的典范名桥——葛镜桥。明万历年间，郡人葛镜宦游归里，以积善为怀，罄尽家资，耗时三十年二毁三建，才终成此桥，遂名"葛镜桥"。

葛镜桥在绝壁之上起拱，借江心一礁石下脚，巧妙运用了自然环境的特点。桥孔顶部微尖，孔距成倍递增，增强了桥梁的承重能力，因此历经四百多年风雨摧折，古桥依然坚固如初，被誉为"西南桥梁之冠"。

桥上倒悬古藤，桥下江流碧绿，青山、河谷和古桥相互映衬，呈现出古朴雄浑的美。四百年弹指一挥间，葛镜桥所沉淀的历史和匠心，在山水中缄默不语，存载着人们将此岸变彼岸的守望，历久弥坚。

The Gejing Bridge, a quintessential bridge in the Chinese history of bridges, was built on the precipice over the banks of the Maha River in the southeast of Fuquan, Guizhou. In the Wanli period of the Ming dynasty, Ge Jing returned to his hometown after retirement. To deliver some charitable deeds, he spent all his wealth on this bridge. The construction spanned thirty years, during which the bridge was destroyed then rebuilt twice. It was named Gejing Bridge after its final completion.

The arch of the Gejing Bridge is made on the precipice starting from a rock in the center of the river, marvelously taking advantage of the characteristics of the natural environment. The top of the bridge arch is slightly sharp and the arch span is in progressive increase, enhancing the bearing capacity of the bridge. Therefore, the ancient bridge is as strong as before despite the weathering over four centuries and is renowned as the "Best Bridge in Southwest China."

With overhanging vines above the bridge and the limpid river under the bridge, green hills, river valleys and the ancient bridge set off each other and exhibit the primitive, imposing beauty. Four hundred years elapsed in a flash, with its history and originality, the Gejing Bridge keeps silent in the landscape, bears people's expectations for communication and is still as steady as before over years.

襄垣永惠桥
The Xiangyuan Yonghui Bridge

　　山西的千年古县襄垣有一座建于金代的古桥——永惠桥，亦称"北关桥"。永惠桥是一座单孔尖拱石桥，它的桥拱初看像是古桥中常见的半圆拱，细看方觉是一个微尖的桥拱。这种桥拱是经典的中国北方桥梁修建技艺之一，也体现了我国古代拱形技术的科技水平。因此这种桥有着较强的承重能力，非常适合古代此地水面交通拥挤且水位较深的河道。

　　桥上青石被岁月打磨得光滑，栏板上雕有奔驰的双马、英武的神牛、灵动的玉兔，以及花卉、麒麟、人物故事等。桥拱顶端装饰着威武的龙首雕塑，怒目圆睁的神龙似乎正欲与激流搏斗，以守一方的水土平安。古桥经历代修缮，保留着金代遗韵、南宋风貌、明清格局，千百年来，无数的行人来来往往，留下了奔忙与叩问的身影。

The Yonghui Bridge, also named Beiguan Bridge, is an ancient bridge built in Xiangyuan County, Shaanxi in the Jinn dynasty and a stone bridge with a single, pointed arch. Its arch looks like the semicircular arch commonly seen in ancient bridges at first glance. Observed carefully, it is a slightly pointed bridge arch. Such a bridge arch is one of the classic bridge building techniques in North China and reflects the advance in arch building in ancient China. Therefore, such bridges boast strong bearing capacities and are suitable for the watercourse of crowded transportation and deep water level here in ancient China.

The bluestones on the bridge are polished smoothly by years. Two dashing horses, valiant bulls, lively rabbits, flowers, Qilin and character stories are engraved on the balustrades. The top of the bridge arch is decorated with the engraving of the head of the martial dragon staring its eyes to fight against the torrents and safeguard the local community. Undergoing repairs in different dynasties, the ancient bridge still maintains the remaining glamour of the Jinn dynasty, the style and features of the Southern Song dynasty and the pattern of the Ming and Qing dynasties. For thousands of years, incalculable pedestrians come to and fro there, hustling around and making inquiries.

23 毓秀桥
The Yuxiu Bridge

毓秀桥位于陕西省韩城，始建于清代康熙年间，是一座石拱十孔桥。桥墩呈梭形，桥底铺以条石，桥面坡缓而悠长，石缝间嵌铁锭加固。石栏的望柱柱头雕刻有各类瓜果或游龙、飞鸟等造型，生动有趣。毓秀桥的每个桥孔的顶部正中各有一石雕龙头，桥两端立有石人坐像，几百年来，这些武弁与神龙一直默默守护着古桥。

毓秀桥雄踞城南，是韩城曾经的交通要道，也是昔日澽水南北唯一的通道，更是过去连接秦晋的咽喉之路。三百年来，世事沧桑，毓秀桥默默卧居水上，雄伟壮美，一切如故。总有游人远道而来，只为站在桥畔，俯瞰桥下潺潺流水，远眺古城风貌。

The Yuxiu Bridge in Hancheng, Shaanxi, which was built in the reign of Emperor Kangxi of the Qing dynasty, is a ten-arch stone bridge, featuring shuttle-shaped piers, stone strips paved bottom, slight but long slopes on the bridge surface and reinforced iron ingot embedded between stone crevices. The heads of the stone balusters are vividly and interestingly engraved with different kinds of vegetables, fruits, flying dragons and birds. There is a stone carving of a dragon's head in the center of the top of each arch of the Yuxiu Bridge, as well as sitting statues of figures erecting on both sides of the bridge. For centuries, these martial figures and fairy dragons have been safeguarding the ancient bridge quietly.

The Yuxiu Bridge lying in the south of the city used to be a vital communication line of Hancheng, the only channel linking the south and north of the Jushui River and the strategic road linking the States of Qin and Jin in the past. The Yuxiu Bridge still lies over the river magnificently as before despite the vicissitudes over three hundred years. Tourists come there from afar simply to stand on the side of the bridge, overlook the gurgling water under the bridge and look at the features of the ancient city in distance.

24 双林三桥
The Shuanglin Three Bridges

湖州双林镇是江南水乡的著名古镇，千百年来，水是这里的命脉和灵魂。水多桥也多，水桥相拥，连接着两岸传统民居，波光桥影，虚实相映，瑰丽多姿。其中，横跨塘河的万元桥、化成桥、万魁桥三座桥已经成为双林镇的文化地标，一道道桥影默数着舟船往来，浸润着游客行人的心事和故事。三座桥均建于明代以前，体量相当，造型基本一致，是典型的江南联拱石桥。从起始的万元桥高耸的中央桥拱中望去，另外两桥身影在其中层层相套，令人惊叹。只有置身其中，方能感知其视觉上的精妙之处。

Shuanglin Town of Huzhou is a noted ancient town in the riverside Jiangnan Region. For thousands of years, water has been the lifeline and soul of that area. Many bridges were built because of so much water there. The water and the bridges embracing each other connect the traditional residences on both banks of the rivers. The glistening light of waves and the shadows of bridges set each other off, full of magnificence. Among them, the Wanyuan Bridge, the Huacheng Bridge and the Wankui Bridge spanning over the Tanghe River have become the cultural landmarks of Shuanglin Town, watching the ships and boats and listening to the mind and stories of the tourists and pedestrians. The three bridges built before the Ming dynasty and of similar volume and shapes are typical stone arcading bridges of the Jiangnan Region. Looking through the towering central arch of the Wanyuan Bridge, you can see the other two bridges and experience the visual wonder personally.

第四章
Chapter 4

静观
Viewing in Still

一 名园胜景中的古桥
Ancient Bridges in Famous Scenic Spots

颐和园中的桥
The Bridges in the Summer Palace

 十七孔桥
The Seventeen-Arch Bridge

  颐和园是中国最后一座皇家园林,也是一座集中华湖山之胜的中国古典园林,更是集南北园林桥梁之大成之作。十七孔桥是颐和园中最大的景桥,长一百五十米,由十七个桥洞组成,横卧于东堤和南湖岛之间,作为颐和园的代表建筑,流露出了皇家园林的非凡气韵。桥上雕饰主次有序,象征权利的狮子,辅以莲花和卷草,望柱雕饰的锦布,则为皇室独享之纹饰。还有桥身的对联,桥旁神兽都用各自的内涵在彰显着皇权的至高无上。

  十七孔桥无论四时晨昏皆有不同美景,更有晴日荡舟、坐雨观湖、雪霁独伫等浪漫的观赏模式,彼时观者或于桥上垂首俯视波澜,或驾一叶扁舟穿柳过桥,如入无声之诗、有形之画。

The Summer Palace, the last royal garden of China, is also a classical Chinese garden representing the best landscape of China and the great accomplishment of the gardens and bridges in both South and North China. The Seventeen-Arch Bridge, a representative architecture of the Summer Palace, exhibits the extraordinary glamour of royal gardens. As the largest scenic bridge in the Summer Palace of a length of 150m and comprising 17 arches, it lies horizontally between the eastern embankment and the South Island. The embellishments are engraved in order on the bridge, including lions symbolizing power, lotuses and curly grass. The brocade cloth used as embellishment engraved on the balusters was ornamentation exclusively used by the royal family. The couplet on the bridge body and the mythical creatures beside the bridge manifest the supreme imperial power with their own connotations.

The Seventeen-Arch Bridge offers different fine views at dawn and dusk which can be appreciated by the viewers in the boat on sunny days, sitting in the rain or standing alone in the snow. At that time, the viewers overlook the great waves on the bridge or cross the bridge in a boat, feeling like they are in a soundless poem or a fantastic picture.

玉带桥
The Jade Belt Bridge

　　玉带桥位于颐和园昆明湖入水口，是一座单孔高拱的汉白玉桥。站在玉带桥上，可俯观昆明湖之水景、抬首仰观万寿山之雄伟，感受皇家园林的磅礴气势与宏大格局。玉带桥与东面的知春桥相对应，互为主景。颐和园中的山水桥梁皆有江南风貌，而玉带桥更是乾隆皇帝对挚爱西湖的移情之所。这位喜好文墨的帝王甚至给此桥留下了"螺黛一痕平铺明月镜，虹光百尺横映水晶帘"的题句。高而薄的桥拱弧线，洁白的汉白玉石材使古桥不辜负其"玉带"美称。半圆的桥洞与水中倒影合璧，如明月玉环穿水而过，充满江南意蕴，更蕴含了中国古典审美中桥与山水人文环境交融统一的精神。

The Jade Belt Bridge at the entrance to the Kunming Lake in the Summer Palace is a single-arch high-arching white marble bridge. Standing on the Jade Belt Bridge, you can overlook the waterscape of the Kunming Lake, look up at the majesty of the Longevity Hill and experience the momentum and grandeur of the royal garden. The Jade Belt Bridge and the Spring-Knowing Bridge in the east set each other off. The mountains, rivers and bridges in the Summer Palace all display the style and features of the riverside towns of the Jiangnan Region while the Jade Belt Bridge is the projection of love of Emperor Qianlong to the West Lake. The emperor fond of writing once autographed the verses "The bridge seems to lie on the mirror-like river, the sunglow looks like a crystal curtain." The high and thin arc of the bridge as well as the white marble materials makes the ancient bridge live up to its reputation as the "Jade Belt." The semicircular bridge arch and its reflection in the water harmoniously look like a jade ring going through the river, full of the mien of the riverside towns of the Jiangnan Region and implying the classical aesthetics of China for integrated landscape, culture and environment.

北海二桥
Two Bridges in Beihai

01 永安桥
The Yong'an Bridge

永安桥位于北京的北海公园中。这片美丽的古代皇家园林曾是几代王朝的帝王御苑。宽阔的水面之中有一座神秘而又美丽的琼华岛，岛上绿荫叠翠间耸立着一座白色佛塔，树木苍郁中隐约可见精致的亭台楼阁。当游人被仙山秘境吸引，急于探访之时，突然发现脚下一座宽阔的石桥如同一条长龙卧于水面，开辟了通向秘境的道路。这座给人惊喜和期待的永安桥，就是这样与白塔合于一处，成了"北海"的标志。桥身有三处曲折，亦有三个桥拱券，桥面铺条石，坡度平缓，使人行于桥上如同行走大道。桥身两侧有雕刻精美的莲花饰望柱和荷叶护栏板。桥南北各立一座华丽的牌坊，枋心有蓝底金字的题额，南为"积翠"，北为"堆云"。坊前各有石狮一对，姿态生动。这些对永安桥极尽奢华的装饰，处处浸润着古代皇家园林中帝王的权威，也使得往来古桥的游人内心升腾起一种肃穆的仪式感。

The Yong'an Bridge lies in the Beihai Park, Beijing. The Beihai Park, which is a gorgeous ancient royal garden, used to be the imperial palace for several dynasties. The mysterious and beautiful Qionghua Island erects in the center of the vast Beihai Lake, a white pagoda stands in the shades of the island, and exquisite pavilions, terrains and towers are visible among verdant trees. When the tourists are attracted by the celestial mountain and mysterious realm and eager to visit it, they will find a broad stone bridge lying on the water like a long dragon and arch up the road to the mysterious realm. The Yong'an Bridge generating surprise and expectations and the

White Tower are the symbols of Beihai. The bridge body has three zigzags and three arches and the bridge surface paved with stone strips has a gentle slope so that the pedestrians walking on the bridge will feel like walking on the thoroughfare. Balusters with exquisitely engraved lotus and guard bars engraved in the design of lotus leaf line both sides of the bridge. An ornate memorial gate stands respectively on the southern and northern side of the bridge, with inscriptions of golden characters on blue background in the center of the square column, "积翠" (accumulation of emerald green) on the southern one and "堆云" (accumulation of clouds) on the northern one. A pair of stone lions erect in front of the square column featuring vivid postures. These extravagant ornaments on the Yong'an Bridge manifest the authority of the emperors in the ancient royal garden and arouse a solemn sense of ceremony in the heart of the visitors touring on the bridge.

02 金鳌玉蝀桥
The Jin'ao Yudong Bridge

北京北海的金鳌玉蝀桥原名金海桥，又叫御河桥，如今俗称"北海大桥"。这座古桥始建于元代，横跨于古代帝王禁苑的北海与中海之间，是中国古老堤障式石拱桥的典范之作。今日的行人若从桥上走过，只觉脚下不过是寻常的沥青道路，若不细看两旁栏杆之下波澜起伏的水面，甚至察觉不到自己已行于桥上，只有荡舟在北海公园宽阔的湖面之上仰望之时，金鳌玉蝀桥古老的身影方才显现。

明代时古桥东西两端分别立有"金鳌""玉蝀"的匾额，故称"金鳌玉蝀桥"。旧时的金鳌玉蝀桥有九个石拱券，每个石拱券顶都有一只吸水神兽的兽头，造型十分华美。原来的古桥望柱均为覆莲柱头，如今为了行人安全已经变成了高高耸起的铁栏。今人初见此景时殊觉遗憾，但细想一番，京华之中多少古桥都已在朝代更迭兴废中化为尘土，这座古桥却依旧屹立如初，仍然肩负着作为桥的功能，用桥身旁的铁栏分割了古老与现代的北京，这种情境却别有一番奇特的感受。

The Jin'ao Yudong Bridge in Beihai, Beijing, originally named Jinhai Bridge and Royal River Bridge, is now commonly referred to as the Beihai Grand Bridge. Built in the Yuan dynasty and spanning over Beihai and Zhonghai, the ancient bridge is a quintessence of stone arch bridge functioning as a dyke in ancient China. The modern pedestrians walking on the bridge may simply feel that it is just an asphalt road. Without watching the rolling water under the balusters on both sides, you may not even realize that you are walking on a bridge. Only when you ride a boat on the vast lake of Beihai Park and look up, will you see the Jin'ao Yudong Bridge.

Once there were two tablets of "金鳌" (jin'ao, golden turtle) and "玉蝀" (yudong, jade rainbow) erected respectively on the eastern and western ends of the ancient bridge in the Ming dynasty, hence its name Jin'ao Yudong Bridge. In ancient times, the bridge had nine stone arches, with each one having a mythical beast head absorbing water and of a resplendent model. The original balusters of the ancient bridge had head in lotus pattern. Now, high iron bars have been erected for the pedestrians' safety. Modern people feel it a pity at this sight. However, on second thought, the ancient bridge still stands as firmly as before and still plays the functions of a bridge although so many bridges in Beijing have vanished during the replacement of dynasties. The iron bars on the bridge separate ancient Beijing and modern Beijing, generating an interesting feeling.

苏州园林诸桥
The Bridges in the Classical Gardens of Suzhou

 九曲桥
The Jiuqu Bridge

苏州西园中有一放生池,池边垂柳如丝,更有一座九曲桥可通湖心亭。此桥虽名"九曲桥",但论其平面,非曲线而为折线。在中国传统园林中常以这种折桥作为景观桥,游人踏上九曲桥后视线随桥的曲折变化移步换景,可于池边静观,也可行于桥上动观其韵,不知不觉间增加了游赏时间。中国园林向来都以自然山水为蓝本,园中景观大多与桥的布局有关,桥若造型突兀、雕缋满眼,则生艳俗之感,且与周围的自然水景格格不入。而眼前这折曲古桥,看似寻常,却将游人行走、静坐的视线牵引至不同的景观。西园景致本不多,但因九曲桥颇显疏密得当,使游人流连忘返。春和景明时,九曲桥栏上,几树紫藤如垂瀑而下,穿紫花飘香而过桥,浪漫之境无以言表,这大约也是古桥每年难得的"抢眼"之时。

There is a freeing life pond in the Xiyuan Temple of Suzhou surrounded by willows. A zigzag bridge leads to the Mid-Lake Pavilion there. Although it was named Jiuqu (nine curves) Bridge, its surface is not in the shape of curves but zigzags. Such zigzag bridges are mostly scenic bridges in traditional Chinese gardens. One step makes the scenes different for the tourists after they step onto these bridges. They can watch quietly beside the pool or walk on the bridge while appreciating its charm, unconsciously spending more time in touring. The natural scenery is always the blueprint of Chinese gardens whose scenes are mostly related with the layout of the bridges. If the bridges were engraved in peculiar models, a sense of gaudiness would be generated, incompatible with the surrounding natural waterscape. The ancient Jiuqu Bridge looks ordinary but attracts the sights of the walking or sitting tourists to different scenes. The Xiyuan Temple does not have many scenes but seems well-proportioned because of the Jiuqu Bridge, which makes the tourists reluctant to leave. On bright sunny days, there are Chinese wistaria cascades on the balusters of the Jiuqu Bridge. Walking on the bridge in the fragrance of these purple flowers, you can feel that the romance is pervasive all over the place. It may be the most appealing moment of the ancient bridge each year.

02 小飞虹
The Small Flying Rainbow Bridge

　　小飞虹位于苏州拙政园，是苏州园林中十分罕见的廊桥。朱栏黛瓦，虽只是微微拱起，便有凌空飞架之势，宛若飞虹之态。古人以"小飞虹"为之命名，堪称绝妙。小桥与水中倒影构成虚实相对的灵动场景，充满了中国古典美学重写意、重意境的审美趣味。

　　古桥连接了池水两岸的曲廊，也丰富了水面的倒影，更分隔了园林两边的空间，却又使两边可以借景相望，这种隔而不绝，使得观者眼中景致空间层次更为深远。池畔叠石嶙峋，古树苍翠，晴日中呈优雅恬静之态，雪雾时现高远超然之姿。在拙政园中古桥连接着历史，塑造着景观的超然品格，成为展现中国古典审美趣味和文化精神的经典范例。

The Small Flying Rainbow Bridge in the Humble Administrator's Garden is a veranda bridge rarely seen in the Classical Gardens of Suzhou. With red balusters, black tiles and slightly arching, it soars aloft like a flying rainbow. The ancients ingeniously named it Small Flying Rainbow Bridge. The bridge and its reflection in the water form a scene of fiction and reality full of the interest of classical Chinese aesthetics focusing on passing the artistic conception.

The ancient bridge links the zigzag verandas on both banks, adds more reflections on the water surface, separates the space on both sides of the garden and makes the scenes face each other. The separation further extends the sense of layers of the scenes. Grotesque stones and verdant ancient trees line beside the pool, producing a sense of gracefulness and serenity on the sunny days and loftiness on snowy days. The ancient bridge in the Humble Administrator's Garden has close ties with history, creating the exceptional character of the scenes and becoming a quintessence of the classical aesthetic interest and cultural essence of China.

03 引静桥
The Yinjing Bridge

中国古代向来有园皆有水，有水皆有桥。桥之于中国古典园林，多半不以交通为要，而是为了连接水陆间的不同景致，并引导游人观览。许多名园景致都是以水池为中心，因此园桥自然要负责起点缀水景，连接假山湖石、亭台水榭之用。

苏州网师园是中国古代园林的典范，其中的引静桥小巧玲珑，三步可逾，简直如同玲珑玉坠般精致。桥身藤萝缠绕，几乎将美丽的牡丹雕饰掩蔽。园中池面较小，环水而建的轩阁廊亭颇多，高拱柔婉的引静桥，使园内布局愈加紧凑。于小桥上观大景，夹岸叠石，池中游鱼戏水、鸭相嬉戏，更觉水池清波灵动，有绵延不尽之感，不禁赞叹造园者的匠心独运。

Water and bridges are indispensable elements of gardens in ancient China. Bridges in classical Chinese gardens are built not for the use of transportation but to link different scenes on water and land and attract tourists. Pools are centers in many famous gardens and therefore bridges in the gardens play the role of embellishing the waterscape and linking artificial hills, lakes, stones, booths, terraces and waterside pavilions.

The Master of the Nets Garden is a quintessence of ancient Chinese gardens. The Yinjing Bridge in the garden is so small that it feels like you can walk across it in three footsteps. It is as exquisite as a small jade pendant. The vine all over the bridge body almost covers the beautiful engraved peonies. The pool in the garden is small and there are many towers, verandas and pavilions surrounding the water. The gentle, high-arch Yinjing Bridge makes the layout of the garden more compact. You can appreciate the grand view on the small bridge with fish swimming and ducks frolicking in the pool. You may feel that the water is clearer and more lively, and extends endlessly. You will absolutely acclaim the ingenuity of the garden builders.

其他桥
Other Bridges

01 庐山观音桥
The Guanyin Bridge in Mount Lu

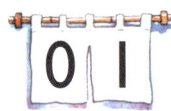

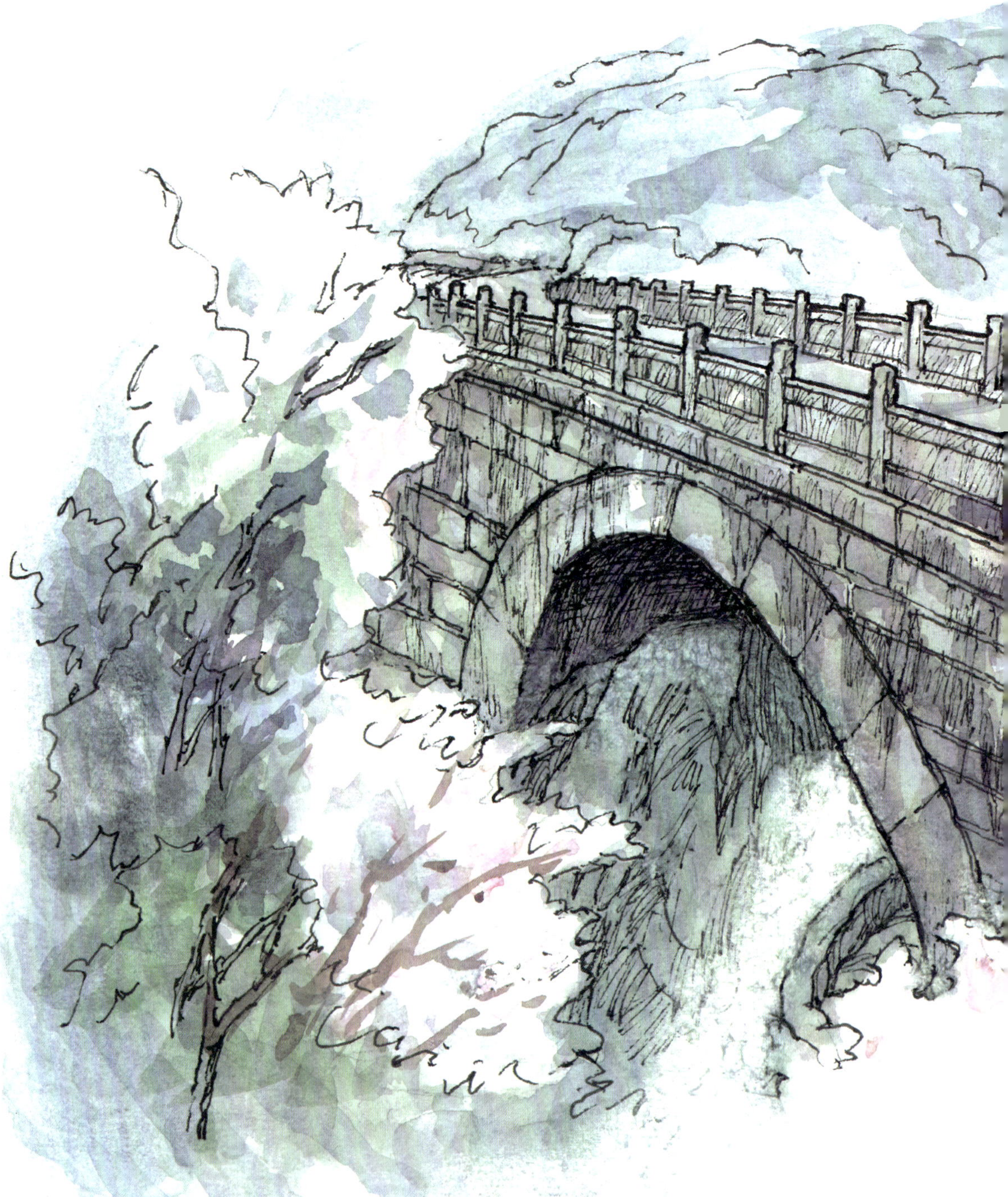

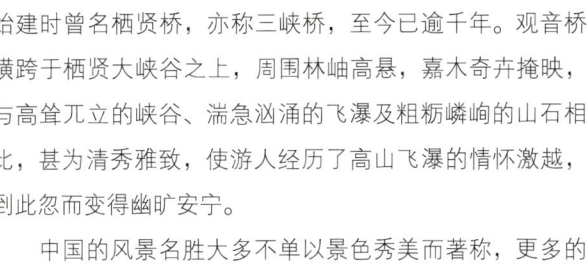

　　观音桥坐落于庐山东南麓，是一座单孔石拱桥，北宋始建时曾名栖贤桥，亦称三峡桥，至今已逾千年。观音桥横跨于栖贤大峡谷之上，周围林岫高悬，嘉木奇卉掩映，与高耸兀立的峡谷、湍急汹涌的飞瀑及粗粝嶙峋的山石相比，甚为清秀雅致，使游人经历了高山飞瀑的情怀激越，到此忽而变得幽旷安宁。

　　中国的风景名胜大多不单以景色秀美而著称，更多的兼具人文情怀、传说掌故，观音桥就是如此。北宋黄庭坚曾作《栖贤桥铭》，文豪苏轼也曾作《栖贤三峡桥》诗，苏辙、杨万里、朱熹、文天祥、唐伯虎等历代文人骚客皆有描绘此桥的诗词丹青流传后世。因此观音桥周身遍是古人题字的摩勒刻石，使我们的思绪在千百年间的中华文脉中穿梭。此时方才明白，以江南古桥之多，为何唯有此桥独享"江南第一古桥"之盛名。

　　The Guanyin Bridge, nestling at the foot of the southeastern Mount Lu, is a single-arch stone bridge, existing for more than 1,000 years. When it was initially built in the Northern Song dynasty, it was called the Qixian Bridge and the Sanxia Bridge. The Guanyin Bridge spans over the Qixian Grand Canyon, with forests lying up in the peak as well as amazing flowers and fine trees cover the ground nearby. Compared with the towering valley, torrential waterfall and coarse and jagged rocks of grotesque shapes, the bridge is handsome and elegant and enables the tourists to feel the serenity and peace after their exaltation for the waterfall in the high mountains.

　　China's scenic spots are not famous just for their splendid scenery but also for their humanistic values, legends and anecdotes. Take the Guanyin Bridge as an example. Men of letters of different dynasties have written poems in praise of the bridge, for instance, Huang Tingjian of the Northern Song dynasty creating "Inscription of the Qixian Bridge," Su Shi of the Northern Song dynasty composing "The Sanxia Bridge," as well as Su Zhe, Yang Wanli, Zhu Xi, Wen Tianxiang and Tang Bohu. Therefore, the Guanyin Bridge features engraved inscriptions by eminent ancients all over and makes our thought shuttle in the Chinese culture over thousands of years. By then you will understand why the Guanyin Bridge enjoys the great reputation as the "No.1 ancient bridge of the Jiangnan Region" despite so many ancient bridges there.

02 曲尺桥
The Quchi Bridge

  曲尺桥，顾名思义桥形如曲折之尺，定然是一座盈尺之间的折桥。这座古桥位于苏州名园环秀山庄中。此园虽小，却揽尽江南之色，尤以湖山叠石著称。此园建筑颇多，水面却不大并且环绕山石呈迂回曲折之状。于是为防夺其势，造园者放弃了常见的如虹高拱的拱桥，而采用了九曲折尺、清雅无痕的折桥来配周围名闻天下的坡渚叠石和半潭秋水。

  中国古典审美趣味偏爱宁静而致远，因此园林中人工属性最强的园桥修造总是最花费心思的。桥在园景中于脚下是观景处，于岸边是景观处，因此无论是借景、造景，都需将人的活动与自然景观相融合，这也彰显出中国古人的自然观和人生观。人立于桥上，脚下碧水缓缓，水至山前绕山而转，人也于桥尽处而下，古朴雄奇的叠石因水而得生机，人因与水同行而生逸趣，这种美虽由人作，但却刚柔相济，有如天工。

  The Quchi (zigzag ruler) Bridge, as its name suggests, is shaped like a zigzag ruler. It is a zigzag bridge in the Mountain Villa with Embracing Beauty, a famous garden in Suzhou. Despite its small size, it offers a panoramic view of the riverside town in the Jiangnan Region and is celebrated for the lakeside stones. There are multitudes of architectures in the garden. However, the lake is not large and the water zigzags around the stones. Consequently, to keep its imposing momentum, the garden builders gave up the practice of building a rainbow-shaped high-arch bridge but an elegant, smooth zigzag bridge to match the stones laying around slopes and pond water widely known to the nation.

  In terms of aesthetic interest, the ancient Chinese prefers serenity and tranquility. Therefore, building the bridge, which has the strongest artificial attributes of the garden, is the most thought-consuming. The bridge is both the place to view the garden and a scene itself in the garden. The efforts of view creating and landscaping need to integrate people's activities with natural scenery, manifesting the conception of nature and outlook on life of the ancient Chinese. Walking on the bridge as the green water flowing underfoot slowly and turning around the stones, the pedestrians will descend at the end of the bridge. The magnificent stones of primitive simplicity are reinvigorated because of the water, and the pedestrians have fun brought by the company of the water. The artificial beauty alternates power with softness and is like the work of nature.

03 虎丘双井桥
The Shuangjing Bridge in Tiger Hill

苏州虎丘美景天下闻名，而虎丘之中最引人入胜的古迹便是被传为吴王阖闾墓的剑池。剑池水质醇美，清澈甘甜，历代都被奉为煮茶汲饮上佳之水。附近云岩禅寺的僧人日常用水也都要去剑池汲取。但是削崖绝壁，山路崎岖，僧人又担水负重，上下山颇感不便。终于在南宋时，一座横跨剑池东西峭壁顶端的木楼建成，并且在水面正上方的楼板处留有两眼，状似井口以便汲水。但木楼渐久倾圮腐朽，于是云岩禅寺方丈便将此处改建为石桥，石桥之上仍留有两个井口状圆洞。这座古桥也遂以"双井桥"之名随虎丘剑池一同闻名于世。行至桥心，桥面上两个不大的圆洞并排而立，透过洞口可见剑池泉水，从来观泉赏池都是极目眺望，而此处却可于方寸之间寻得，如同一张盈尺古画，给游人别样的盎然意趣。

    The name of Tiger Hill of Suzhou spreads over the world and the most intriguing historical site is the Sword Pond which is said to be the tomb of King He Lv of Wu. The water in the pond is mellow, limpid and sweet and has been praised to be the best water for making tea throughout the history. In ancient times, the monks of the Yunyan Temple nearby went to fetch water from the pond to use regularly. However, due to the precipice and rugged mountain roads, the monks felt it burdensome to carry the heavy water uphill and downhill. Finally, a wooden building was built spanning the eastern and western precipices of the Sword Pond. Two holes of the floorslabs were left right above the water surface like the mouth of a well to draw water. Nonetheless, the wooden building inclined and got decayed. Therefore, the Buddhist abbot of the Yunyan Temple had it rebuilt into a stone bridge, still leaving two round holes like two wells in the stone bridge. The ancient bridge became famous as the Shuangjing (two wells) Bridge together with the Sword Pond in Tiger Hill. Walking to the bridge center, you can see two ordinarilysized round holes erecting side by side on the bridge surface and the spring water of the Sword Pond through the mouth of the holes. It is common to look afar to appreciate springs and ponds elsewhere but you can find the poetic, distinctively interesting scene only in this small scenic area.

Ancient Chinese Bridges

Written by Guan Wei and Shen Xiaolei

Illustrated by Cai Pinchun

First English Edition 2023

By China Pictorial Press Co., Ltd.

CHINA INTERNATIONAL COMMUNICATIONS GROUP

Copyright © China Pictorial Press Co., Ltd.

All rights reserved.

No part of this publication may be reproduced, stored in a retrieval system, or transmitted in any form or by any means, electronic, mechanical, photocopying, recording, or otherwise, without the prior written permission of China Pictorial Press Co., Ltd., except for the inclusion of brief quotations in an acknowledged review.

Address: 33 Chegongzhuang Xilu, Haidian District, Beijing, 100048, China

ISBN 978-7-5146-2067-2